Blue Plums on a Mat of Leaves

Ponderings at Break of Day

Charles C. Finn

Chapin Keith Publishing
Daleville, VA. 24083

Publisher's Cataloging-in-Publication Data

Names: Finn, Charles C. Finn, author.
Title: Blue Plums on a Mat of Leaves / Charles C. Finn

Identifiers: LCCN: 2023902992 | ISBN 978-1-7344807-5-7 (Paperback) |
978-1-7344807-6-4 (eBook)
BISAC POETRY / General | POETRY/ American/General

Cover and book design by Asya Blue Design

Front cover: Photo by Charles C. Finn

First Edition

Visit the author's website at https://poetrybycharlescfinn.com/

DEDICATED

to seekers everywhere
assured on high authority
if we seek we will find.

CONTENTS

AUTHOR'S FOREWORD

⌒

Before the busyness of the day takes over (even in retirement a to-do list is always waiting), I begin the day before fire. From autumn to spring it's the flaming in a woodstove; from spring to autumn it's the fire of the rising sun viewed from a circle of stones in a cathedral of trees. After a ritual of remembering, I wait for things to come with pad in lap and pen in hand. Some of those things are in this volume. I variously think of them as ruminations, revelations, gifts from the mysterious blue. Having the conviction that the reader and I are more like than we are unlike, I want to scatter these gifts like seeds to the wind. One of my wisdom figures (many will appear in the offerings to follow) caught it perfectly.

"The plums, like some gift given from no one to no one visible, continued to fall about me. I was old now, I thought suddenly, glancing at a vein on my hand. I would have to hoard what remained of the embers...for my own head was growing weary and the smoke from the autumn fields seemed to be penetrating my mind. I wanted to drop them at last, these carefully hoarded memories. I wanted to strew them like the blue plums in some gesture of love toward the universe all outward on a mat of leaves. Rich, rich and not to be hoarded, only to be laid down for someone, anyone..." (Loren Eiseley, *The Unexpected Universe*, 231-2)

These "blue plums" are to be taken slowly, in the same pondering mood as they were written. Though they proceed chronologically, covering a full year picking up in March of 2021 where *Who's to Say*

Every *Bush is Not Burning?* left off, they need not be read that way. A more intuitive approach might be to glance through the Table of Contents and follow the lure of an intriguing title that invites you to come see. These poems might have appeal particularly to those who recognize themselves to be on a spirit journey. For those curious as to what a spirit journey encompasses, the answer is everything.

INTRODUCTION

⟋

This collection of recent poems begins on a serious note, reflecting the heavy news my wife and I had just received. As will be seen throughout, my practice is to stay in the moment, pondering what happens to be crossing my mind or the news, stirring my heart or my memory. Readers will recognize how quickly the moment changes, triggering ever new reflections and memories. That certain themes keep recurring suggests important findings from a long journey.

Out of the blue came very dark clouds in the form of a call from our daughter. All we could do was brace ourselves.

Please Not, Fearful Hearts Plead

They're keeping Brewster in the hospital
to do a bone marrow biopsy.
Thankfully his spirits are up--
able to watch TV non-stop!
His mother right beside him
and his father flying back from Colorado
are having a far more difficult time
keeping their own spirits up
ever since April was told in the ER
to get him right away to a pediatric oncologist.
Grandparents with hearts in their throats
await the results of the biopsy
before heading to Tennessee.
Dark clouds out of the blue.
Please not, fearful hearts plead. 3/13/21

My wife's words caught it.

Terrified

"I'm terrified at what we might learn today,"
was all she could say sobbing.
My arms around her
was all I could respond. 3/14/21

My own words in the form of a poem, more like a prayer.

Be the Presence that Holds Us Together

God of all of our hearts,
be the Presence that holds us together
through dark days ahead.
We are about to learn the kind of leukemia
which will determine the treatment needed.
A tough road ahead for a bright boy of five,
likely a tougher road ahead
for two whose love for him is boundless
making them vulnerable to every fear.
Help us all remember, force of love within us,
source of light around us,
that what binds us together will see us through,
that a little boy facing a rigorous journey
never alone will make it through. 3/14/21

Down to Basics.

One Thing is for Certain

As trusting as we try to be,
it seizes the heart to hear "leukemia"
imagining his ordeal ahead.
One thing is for certain--
this boy of five building Legos in his dreams
has surrounding him a cohort of angels. 3/15/21

A lullaby softly returns.

Cradled

"Like a ship in the harbor,
like a mother and child,
light a light in the darkness
I'll hold you a while.
We'll rock on the waters,
I'll cradle you deep
and hold you while angels
sing you to sleep."
As I sang this years ago
to a little girl in my arms
I sing it to her still
and now to her own little one
undergoing surgery at the moment
cradled in all of our arms. 3/15/21

Politics creeps in.

Better Ignorant than Hard of Heart

The ignorant
can be helped by history and literature,
the hard of heart by nothing
except possibly religion. 3/17/21

A different lullaby to his sister.

For Mari to Remember

May this girl of two
easing toward sleep
secure that Pop Pop is near
be reminded some later day by this poem
(more like a little prayer)
that on the strength of the love
for the granddaughter of his heart
she can be secure whenever easing toward sleep
that even when he can't be seen
Pop Pop will be there. 3/26/21

A thunderclap on Lookout Mountain.

Taking It In

"Rain and thunder, wind and fire"—
a perfect mantra for the morning.
Rain lashing,
wind thrashing,
flag snapping,
chimes flinging out broad their names,
bird not cowed into silence--
I swear I heard Mockingbird in the din!
Bundled to keep warm on the porch swing
while others still slept,
I gloried to remember it all starting
with a thunderclap jolting me upright,
insisting I go out to take it in--
which I'm now doing! 3/29/21

*Pondering that night in Gethsemane, as much on those
scattering as on the one rooted.*

Searing Conversation

Since they all fled the Garden
leaving him to face it alone,
the fact that not a single one remained
to overhear his pleading
in no way invalidates the searing conversation
that being human he must have had
with the one he called Father. 4/2/21

And as for those fleeing...

Anguished companions
in the hearts of those fleeing—
terror, guilt, and grief. 4/2/21

And then that brutal next day.

Jesus Hanging from a Lynching Tree

Pondering the Friday called Good,
I can't help but wonder what the stirring would be,
the pained revelation,
were the object of our veneration
be Jesus hanging not from a cross
but a lynching tree.
Were this to wrench us awake,
would that, too, not be good
on this Friday insisting we look closer
than some distant far away? 4/2/21

Crushing news forces new discovery.

Not Insignificant Discoveries

When tough things happen
we find out two amazing things—
how many people are behind us
and how much strength lies within us.
Not insignificant discoveries
when tough things happen. 4/5/21

Here I am pondering what is it about Hemingway
that fails to pull me in.

An Oldster Still on the Track

As I begin watching a new Hemingway documentary
I'll be figuring out what it is
about him and his work that fail to pull me in.
Call it an oldster still on the track
of understanding what makes himself tick.
Sometimes the strongest clues
come from understanding what doesn't. 4/9/21

*For how to end conflicts with honor, do we not have
exemplars in Grant and Lee?*

That Commanding Word Honor

It was today at Appomattox
one hundred plus fifty-six years ago
that it virtually ended,
the war coming close to ripping America asunder.
How both generals handled themselves and their men
commends them.
It has everything to do
with that commanding word honor.
Check the record and see. 4/9/21

*We appreciate something, Chesterton kept reminding,
when we realize it can be lost.*

Architectural Miracle

Is anything more astounding
than the architecture of the brain,
the miracle of its smooth functioning?
I took it for granted
until the removal of a life-threatening tumor
from the brain of our close neighbor
leaves me longing for the return to smooth functioning
of the architectural miracle of his brain. 4/10/21

The opening line of "Felix Randal," poem by Gerard Manley Hopkins, captures a healing truth.

Bringing out the Best in Us

"This seeing the sick endears them to us, us too it endears."
Hopkins begins with a recognition
in his eulogy for an ailing blacksmith
that visiting one gravely ill
brings out the best in us both.
His heart went out to the suffering--
was not that the mark of Jesus?
Seeing others laid low so endears them to us
that our best instinct is to reach out
either with helping hand up close
or prayer for comfort and courage from afar.
But us too it endears.
Our heart-response to another laid low
makes us dear.
We need only remember grateful eyes
for some token of our kindness,
for our simple presence.
Thanks for the reminder, GMH,
that giving comfort to the sick endears them to us,
us too endears. 4/14/21

This is not the whole picture, but can it be denied?

A Vale of Tears

A vale of tears,
captured by Virgil's "lacrimae rerum," (the tears of things)--
is it not that for us all,
at one point or another and always at the end
saying farewell to every last one?
A friend feels broken after yet another assault,
would like to disappear on a mountain.
My grandson, home but for a week from the hospital,
is headed back with a sudden infection.
Yet another police killing of an unarmed Black.
Abe and Mary, 156 years ago to the day,
lifted up by the war's imminent end,
prepared after a carefree carriage ride
for an evening's relaxation at the theater.
A vale of tears. 4/14/21

How not feel compassion for Mary Lincoln?

Can We Wonder She was Broken?

His breathing was becoming shallow,
coming soon would be the end.
Consigned to an outer room
("Get that hysterical woman out of here!")
she was prevented from even holding his hand.
Another Mary at least was allowed
to hear the tortured last gasp of her son
at the foot of a cross long ago.
Can we wonder that for the rest of her life
Mary Todd Lincoln was broken? 4/15/21

Morning ritual in leafy cathedral.

How Better Begin a Day or End a Life?

I end a morning ritual in my own Chartres
how I hope to end my life,
dancing like a dervish whirling
with no less partners than Sun and Earth!
To see me from a distance
you'd think it was just some old guy
doing slow-motion jumping jacks
revolving clockwise till reaching a solstice point,
then counter-clockwise on the return.
But what's really going on is Eagle
first sailing West on the path of Golden Sun,
then sailing serenely back
honoring Earth's incessant Eastward turn.
Beginning a day or ending a life,
how better than saluting Sun and Earth
on the wings of Eagle? 4/18/21

*A musing on how we might become, as we age, like
a little child again.*

The Tallest of Tall Invitations

When life breaks you down
but you find the courage
to abandon all pretense and admit it,
how have you not by embracing again vulnerability
become like a little child?--
refreshing from the spontaneous young,
inspiring from the courageous old.
Hear in "become like the little children"
the tallest of tall invitations
once again to embrace vulnerability
after a very long journey. 4/18/21

*Blacks were braced for the Dream to be deferred yet again,
but thankfully not this time.*

To the Relief of a Nation

George Floyd's killer
on all three counts was found guilty
to the relief of a nation
holding to hope's slimmest thread
that the dream of "justice for all"
when it comes to crime White against Black
this time is not dead. 4/21/21

On the passing of a regal presence, Arthur Fink.

The Passing of Arthur

The reference to a long ago king
takes on poignant new meaning
for those whose lives have been touched
by the prodigious creativity and compassion
of a kingly man whose round table
encompassed the whole world.
It is we who will rest in peace
when remembering Friend Arthur. 4/25/21

Something to remember when grieving.

Lantern in the Night

Someone passing from our midst
who has been a comfort to many,
an inspiration to many,
a lantern in the night to many,
can truly be said,
carried now in the hearts of many,
not to have passed at all. 4/26/21

It made my day.

From Deflated to Elated

Heavy of heart for days
to see a single goose on our pond
imagining him grieving the loss of his mate,
today I was elated to see two adult geese
proudly strutting above said pond
with four goslings bobbing behind them!
The light bulb flashed--
instead of a grieving mate
he had been an expectant father! 4/26/21

This was prompted by the opening lines of a Mary Oliver poem enti-
tled "When": "When it's over it's over, and we don't know, any of us,
what happens then, so I try not to miss anything..."

Live in Dread or Smile Instead

Not one of us knows for a fact
when the final curtain will fall
or what happens then
so do we live in dread of the unknown
or smile instead at the utter gratuity
of the wonder-filled day before us?
Remembering Mary Oliver
may we try not to miss anything. 4/27/21

We could sing of friendship for a thousand years and have only begun singing.

On Wind Chimes and Friends

Sitting on the porch on an April afternoon
with chimes announcing Wind's living presence,
I'm struck by a resounding recognition--
is this not what friends are in essence,
chimes making music in our lives
each ringing out uniquely
Spirit's living presence? 4/27/21

I love when a quote leaps out at me like a brigand from the bush. I thank G. K. Chesterton for the image.

Safe inside His Voice

"He made you feel safe inside his voice."
This tribute to Tony Bennett
catches perfectly the counselor's hope,
the comforter's hope,
the friend's hope,
the hope of any leaning toward love.
The journey of your life has been golden
if others feel safe inside your voice. 5/5/21

The reference in the following is to Alan Paton's anguished commentary on South Africa's system of apartheid.

Haunting Lamentations

⟿

Reading in *400 Souls:*
A Community History of African America, 1619-2019
of this nation's disgrace too troubling to face
calls to mind *Cry, The Beloved Country,*
a haunting lamentation from another sorrowful time,
from another sorrowful place. 5/7/21

The fact that chance winds are always blowing in no way negates the possibility of meaning.

It's What You Choose to Do with It

⟿

It's not that it was meant to be,
what you are now facing--
thanks to chance it simply is.
What you choose to do with it
will *make* the meaning. 5/8/21

Clearer and clearer it's becoming, not only who participated in the insurrection but why.

They Will Not Replace Us!

"Fear of the great replacement"--
that the rights of Blacks and Hispanics
are outpacing the rights of Whites--
was the most significant common denominator
found in those so far arrested
in the insurrection of January 6.
That 86% were male,
many having served in the military,
might, with demographic change unstoppable,
be very good reason to worry. 5/8/21

I remember from long ago a sentence with piercing, sudden-again relevance.

A Powerful Odor of Mendacity

Burl Ives playing Big Daddy
in the movie *Cat On A Hot Tin Roof*
had a blockbuster of a line:
"There's a powerful odor of mendacity in this room!"
What happens when mendacity's stench
becomes noxiously evident
not in a room but a nation? 5/9/21

Mothers Day invites wider imagination.

Way to Go, Heroic Forebears!

Hear "myths," think "stories,"
some foundational.
Way to go, Adam, for the daring
to taste the fruit of the tree of knowledge--
could we have risen to love without it?
Way to go, Eve, for cajoling him into it
thanks to your greater attunement
to the whispering in your ear.
Way to go, wise serpent,
literally in touch with the wisdom
of our divinely-grounded Mother. 5/9/21

May mothers
not excluding Earth
receive today thanks from their children. 5/9/21

Reimagining the crucifixion as a lynching brings it closer to home, intensifies the shudder.

A Look that You Can't Shake

Just imagine being in the crowd
gawking at a lynching
and hearing before the rasping last gasp
unsettling words about forgiveness,
and damned if he doesn't find your eye
for a penetrating last look
that for the life of you you can't shake. 5/10/21

To the degree we love, we know grieving.

Out of Sight is not out of Heart

This is not to assuage you from your tears
for if anything is holy it is tears,
rather it is simply to remind you
that out of sight is not out of heart.
Hearts bound by love are beyond unbounding. 5/17/21

Looking over your life, what have been your greatest
sources of wisdom?

Wisdom Sources

At a certain felicitous time
I identified my greatest sources of wisdom--
natural world,
ancestors accompanying,
worlds of literature and art,
Catholic foundation, Quaker synthesis,
amazing synchronicities,
dismaying disruptions.
Those puzzling at the inclusion of disruptions
might look to the range of revelations
stemming from disruptions of their own. 5/18/21

It's hard to shut out the world, even when gardening.

Poppies and Peonies and War

Poppies and peonies are peaking--
such color, such fragrance--
can it be anything but spring?
Then a sting
remembering some are having this moment
to leave their poppies and peonies
and everything else held dear behind
in a desperate rush to escape with their lives. 5/20/21

Pondering the bravery needed to break free from a lie.

Not Counting out the Possibility

Will they ever admit
the Lie's in fact a lie?
While I'm not holding my breath,
neither am I counting out the possibility
of late bursts of conscience and courage. 5/21/21

Try the following to remind you how rich you are.

Wealthy in What Matters

Place names on a page
of those dear to your heart,
then let the names become faces--
each set of eyes
meeting yours with an exchange
of great gratitude for the gift
of your abiding mutual presence.
Lacking all else,
would not you consider yourself rich? 5/22/21

*Think the last time someone held your gaze while saying
something important.*

Straight into My Eyes

When one you admire
both for his or her heart and spirit-savvy
looks you straight in the eyes
and says "I am proud of you,"
you remember it like it was yesterday
even if 43 years later.
Beyond words of deep validation
that each hungers to hear,
it was that look straight into my eyes. 5/23/21

"It's just another day." Hardly.

Listening for Today's Call

Can you hear the call
on this new day in your life
once again to muster up courage?
To do what? you may innocently ask
until you settle into stillness
to hear today's call. 5/23/21

Some memories are etched.

Still Listening

34 years ago this morning
after recounting to a Native guide
my experience while crying for a vision,
I was given the name Tree Listener.
Sitting now in my oak and hickory cathedral
waiting for sunrise I'm continuing to listen. 5/24/21

I love the metaphor of the mansion with many rooms.

Each Room has a Voice

Guilt from least provocation
booms from the basement, "Lazy coward!"
Thankfully other voices sound
from sunnier rooms up higher. 5/24/21

No wonder Memory was the first of the Muses.

The Right Place in All the World

Thirteen years ago this day
my eagle brother and I stood in silence
at the bustling corner between White House and Soldiers'
Home
where a shaggy-bearded, barbaric-yawping bard
waited to tip his homespun hat
to a revered one passing
of whom he'd cry on a shrouded day coming,
"O Captain, My Captain."
It felt the right place in all the world
for eagle brothers amidst the bustle of DC
to stand in silence. 5/24/21

Imagine yourself a Druid on the subject of trees.

In a Living Tree's Presence

Stretching ecstatically for Father,
rooted firmly in Mother,
bending submissively to winds of Spirit,
arms welcoming all manner of fellow creature--
how not be inclined to bow head, lift heart,
in a living tree's presence? 5/24/21

The reference is to The Hobbit. Let's just say I identify with Bilbo.

Are We not Each a Reluctant Warrior?

What consternation was Bilbo's
when Gandalf disrupted his comfortable existence
by sweeping him up into adventures
for which he was convinced he lacked the courage.
Confounding this diminutive hobbit further
was the wizard's repeated assertion to others,
"There is more to Mr. Baggins than meets the eye."
Are we not each a reluctant warrior
when a wizard sweeps in from nowhere
and knocks on our door? 5/25/21

Michelangelo long gone? I beg to differ.

Right Here, Right Now

According to teachers of wisdom across the planet,
right here is the right place,
right now is the right time
for each to be Michelangelo
imagining what David might be hidden
in the white marble next moment. 5/24/21

I know it's heresy to question God's omniscience, but what if?

What If

Consider that God has never been here before
facing what you now are facing.
What if He were as curious as you
wondering what it is together
the two of you will do next?
What if She were no less hopeful than you
that love will inform what together
the two of you will do next? 5/25/21

Revisiting Moby Dick after barely surviving an Ahab at the helm.

What a Yarn Melville Spun

What a fairy tale is *Moby Dick*!
No captain in his right mind
would hunt truth to the death
at risk of ship and crew being dragged to the bottom.
O what a yarn Melville spun. 5/26/21

Would that the Crew Resisted

Would that the crew resisted
Ahab's suicidal attempt to slay truth
lest truth return with savage justice
to take to the locker of Davy Jones
not only vengeance-crazed captain
but timorous-cowed crew. 5/26/21

It's Hard to Know

It's hard to know whom to pity more--
the captain in monomaniacal pursuit
of the truth he would slay
or those mindlessly clinging to his lie
sure to sink with him when truth charges back
to batter the doomed ship to bits. 5/27/21

An Allegorical Warning

Think of the tale
of the great white whale
as an allegory forever warning
against savage blind pursuit
to slay Leviathan Truth. 5/27/21

I started with whales, but then imagination took over.

Invite Imagination

Sounding ocean depths--
I am Whale!
Riding high thermals--
I am Eagle!
Fire at volcanic heart--
I am Earth!
Ecstatic answer to Love's lightning--
I am Thunder!
Invite imagination
to see beneath and beyond
the face in the mirror. 5/28/21

Candidate for the most-needed slogan:
LIES ARE HAZARDOUS TO YOUR HEALTH.

When We Buy into a Lie

What happens to our soul
when we buy into a lie,
whether our own or another's?
Does not each deep down know
in excruciating exactitude? 5/28/21

If we had been spared the great lament of 2016, would we not plausibly have faced an even greater in 2020? Here's an invitation to conjecture.

If You Think We're in a Pickle Now

It's not hard to imagine
had Hillary won in 2016
Trump pulling the same stunt—
had he not ahead of the election
insisted it would be rigged against him?
With a Republican Congress staunchly opposing
and the "Lock her up!" drumbeat rising,
not only would her every move have been thwarted
but had she *not* been locked up
it's not a hard stretch to imagine
a storming of the very Capitol!
When 2020 then rolled around,
who do you think would be waiting in the wings
to Make White America Great Again?
If you think we're in a pickle now,
imagine the pickle then. 5/31/21

*Hopkins is ever in the wings. It comes from what feels
a lifetime together.*

And Glow, Glory in Thunder

Clouds darken,
wind is up,
sky and trees confirm what forecasters warn—
a storm approaches!
I thrill to it,
sitting here in my circle of stones with ancestors
surrounding,
none more than Hopkins whose voice still sounds,
"And glow, glory in thunder!"
What do they know those claiming he's gone? 5/28/21

Eiseley is another one front and center for me, ever since I was prompted by a Thomas Berry tape to check him out. The Unexpected Universe is where I started, then to The Immense Journey, then there was no stopping. It happens when you've been opened to vastness.

Think Not Literal Starfish

Yield to Loren Eiseley's "Star Thrower,"
but think not literal starfish--
rather the passion at the root of the cosmos
that against astronomical odds
keeps flinging life forward,
inviting as did Jesus
fellow flingers to follow. 5/29/21

Creating the narrative of a noble cause thwarted only by superior might has effectively blocked necessary grieving. The Big Lie now being trumpeted is not the first.

Questioning Judgment Dishonors not Valor

Questioning the judgment of those who fought for the Confederacy
is not to dishonor the memory of their valor.
What is turning them now in their graves
is the slowness of their proud descendants
to find the requisite courage for healing
by acknowledging their forebears' misjudgment
when justifying the upheavals of secession and war
in order to maintain the system of Black backs
undergirding the life that they knew. 5/29/21

The more you know of Teilhard de Chardin, the more minstrel fits.

Hear an Earth Minstrel Singing

A universe lit from within and still birthing--
vision cast to the winds
by a mystic-hearted minstrel of Earth
spying Spirit behind both science and religion.
Before you try pigeonholing Teilhard,
hear him singing! 5/29/21

Who says syrup isn't a fitting subject for a poem?

When Putting Ample Syrup on Waffles

Rather than berating myself this morning
for yielding yet again to the sweet tooth temptation,
I'll sing instead a little song
about the miraculous transmutation of sweetness
from the colossus of a generosity-fueled star
to the sap-tapping from standing maples
to my gratefully tasting tongue. 5/29/21

Or moths?

Drawn by the Light

No sooner had I turned on the lamp
than moths drawn by the light
appeared at the window--
a four in the morning reminder
of kin fluttering in the night
like me just waiting for light. 5/31/21

Once I start singing of Loren Eiseley, it's hard to stop.

Inviting Awe at the Face in the Mirror

"Beyond lies the great darkness of the ultimate Dreamer
who dreamed the light and the galaxies.
Before act was, or substance existed,
imagination grew in the dark"--
invitation from Loren Eiseley
to bow before the magnitude of the mystery
not only of the Ultimate Imaginer
but of its embodiment in the face in the mirror!
"Man partakes of that ultimate wonder and creativeness...
We are in a creative universe.
Let us then create." 5/31/21

Whimsically serious.

Cracking the Bullfrog Code

Three dozen exact years ago
I cracked the bullfrog code.
Back and forth from around our pond
bullfrogs were having at it--
bringing to me music but not comprehension
until it struck like lightning
that what they were in fact announcing
was the mystic's manifesto!
To each croak of NOW
came the response across the pond WOW,
telling it like it is to one fit to explode
having at last cracked the code! 6/5/21

I suddenly found myself thinking of my father.

This Twinkle in His Eye

The gift of my father--
coming to me this morning
as birds are announcing the spreading light--
was his whimsy,
let out whenever an opportunity
for a pun presented itself.
He'd then have this twinkle in his eye
waiting for you to get it and groan.
I'm not sure what brought him to mind--
perhaps the whimsical birds,
perhaps the twinkling light. 6/8/21

Imagine eye-twinkling God
waiting to see if and when
we'll get it. 6/8/21

Want proof of immortality? Think of any beloved poet.

And Good Morning to You, Mary Oliver

Think of it--
a little closer and we'd fry,
a little further and we'd freeze.
Talk about being at just the right time
in just the right place!
Mary Oliver in "Why I Wake Early"
caught it perfectly in her song to the sun:
"Best preacher that ever was,
dear star, that just happens
to be where you are in the universe
to keep us from ever-darkness,
to ease us with warm touching,
to hold us in the great hands of light--
good morning, good morning, good morning."
And good morning to you, Mary Oliver,
decidedly still with us. 6/8/21

A consideration when tempted to throw in the towel.

Taking Heart from Those Most Assaulted

When dismay borders on alarm
at the resurgence of White supremacy
threatening to deluge with fascist flooding,
I take heart from those most assaulted--
Natives and Jews against designs of extermination
and Black backs harnessed to the merciless plow
for the sake of the birth of a nation.
If these have survived bigotry's brutality and bruising,
losing neither faith nor resolve,
then the last thing I have justification for doing
when dismay borders on alarm
is losing either faith or resolve.
I'd have to answer if I do
to the likes of Crazy Horse, John Lewis,
and Ruth Bader Ginsberg. 6/9/21

David Attenborough is less a British treasure than an Earth treasure, the prophet-mentor we desperately need.

Seldom More Admiration, Seldom More Fear

Seldom have I felt more admiration
than when listening to a passionate Earth warrior
still fighting at 95 for our grandchildren
and all children after.
Seldom have I felt more fear
than when listening to this warrior's assessment
of our global climate crisis.
If David Attenborough can't shout us awake
to our home on the brink of catastrophe,
pray God who can? 6/10/21

A Crying Shame

A crying shame--
the phrase stabs with new meaning
when realizing what we mindlessly are doing
to the mother that bore us. 6/10/21

A clue into why the name John for me is incandescent.

Diamond John

Grandfather,
father,
brother,
nephew,
spirit father,
eagle brother,
wolf brother,
mystic evangelist,
pope throwing open Vatican windows,
intrepid biblical guide,
irrepressible Celtic bard,
poet of heart and imagination,
Yosemite champion.
O the facets for me flashing
off the diamond name John. 6/11/21

The absolute calm in the eye of the storm is a remarkable thing.
Think on it.

The Hurricane's Sermon

When a personal whirlwind bears down,
remember the hurricane's sermon:
Find your way to the eye
where you'll hear the voice in the calm
instilling encouragement and trust
as you ride out the storm. 6/15/21

Ah, that illusion of separateness.

In Fact I am Populated

I may seem alone out here
in my stone circle in the woods,
but in fact I am populated--
cloud of witnessing ancestors,
childhood phantoms persisting,
friends of the heart never absent,
notions pleading Just imagine,
intimations pleading Write us down!
What an assembly!
Deep down isn't every "I"
truly a population?
I'm reminded of Whitman, Rumi, and Hafiz
celebrating and singing themselves
along with their populations. 6/17/21

Some like to start with the comics, I like to end with them--an amiable way to embark on a hopefully amiable day.

An Amiable Way to Embark on the Day

Baby Blues catches impish childhood,
Zits adolescent quirkiness,
Pickles the whimsies of aging.
Then there is atrocious punning in Pearls Before Swine,
wisdom of Frazz and wackiness of Agnes,
boy-dog tenderness between Red and Rover,
and of course beloved standbys--
Dagwood and Dennis and good old gullible Charlie Brown
with Snoopy's nearby dervish dancing.
While some may seek escape when turning to the comics,
I seek reminders of humor's sanity
across the panoply of humanity,
even if the price is a groan
at an atrocious pun. 6/17/21

Variations on a theme.

First Shame, Then Courage

How without courage
born of essential shame
can America redeem grievances
centuries seething? 6/19/21

Facing the Truth of a Wrong

Perhaps what is hardest
about facing the truth of a wrong
is not only allowing shame to awaken
but then finding the requisite courage
to begin righting the wrong. 6/19/21

Sometimes upon hearing a quote, it feels a seed was planted.

"The Earth and I are of One Mind"

Such a word, MIND--
how we have narrowed it to pipsqueak proportions
limiting it to just humans.
Think of every particle in the universe
as a spark flying from the SINGLE BLAZING MIND.
Listen to how they held to it,
the first to Turtle Island:
"The Earth and I are of one mind."
The tree outside your window,
the laboring ants--
what intelligence,
how are we not kin? 6/23/21

Another seed, this time from Tennyson.

A Part of All That I Have Met

On the brink of sailing beyond the sunset
across the final sea
Tennyson's *Ulysses* exclaimed,
"I am a part of all that I have met."
Not all is part of me
but I am part of all!
Think what you will leave behind
as you embark on your journey beyond the sunset
across the final sea. 6/23/21

There they go again, impugning America's character!

The House of America

Would Blacks be welcome in your neighborhood,
in your church,
at your table,
in your family?
If not pray tell why not,
you who claim racism in the US
is not baked into White bones.
Such bright parlor has the house of America,
such dark basement. 6/25/21

Garden lovers will understand this one. Back from my morning jog
to get the paper, I saw with dismay the damage.

When You Give Your Life over to Beauty

Know what you're in for
when you give your life over to beauty.
My wife's love for her daylily garden
dubbed by me Penny's Paradise
is far beyond reach of mere words
as will be her devastation this morning
to see the damage wrought,
the countless bulging buds consumed,
by an intruder in the night
hungry enough to brave flaming wire.
Words won't even try to console
but arms will do their best
to encircle her sorrow. 6/25/21

The passage is from "The Wreck of the Deutschland" in which a Jesuit seminarian, back in 1875, was asked by his superior to write a few words following a tragic loss at sea.

A Way of Taking off His Shoes

"Beyond saying sweet, past telling of tongue,
Thou art lightning and love, I found it, a winter and warm;
Father and fondler of heart thou hast wrung:
Hast thy dark descending and most art merciful then."
The poet Hopkins had a way with words,
a way of taking off his shoes
in the presence of that greatest of all mysteries
after the birth of the universe--
evil somehow embedded
in the goodness of God. 6/26/21

I remember nothing from the novel Forsyte Saga except a single line. Let's just say, looking back sixty years, it must have touched something core.

Love Aided and Abetted by Death

"What is it makes us love and makes us die?"
Could it be that consciousness of the latter
more than anything else in the world
is what aids and abets the former? 6/28/21

Reading Carl Jung's Answer to Job is not for the faint of faith.

Pondering Your Place on This Planet

Thinking of Jung's thunderous thesis
that Job helped to humanize God
suggests that we each can be an extension
of God's continuous birthing!
Sit with that a stunned moment
as you ponder your place on this planet
journeying around a generous sun. 6/26/21

"Ho-hum, it's just another day." Are you kidding?

On the Edge of My Seat

What amazing thing will I hear today
that will rush up,
seize me by the coat collar and shout,
"This is it, dummy, this is why you're here!"
or see today that will blow me away,
or feel today that will melt me or ignite me?
What drama to be on the edge of my seat
awaiting revelation? 6/30/21

Relax on your porch with a new metaphor for God.

Held in God's Hammock

How firmly we are held in the hammock of God.
There is no need to wait for a sweet chariot
to swing low to carry us home
when we swing and sway to the realization
that even as our journey through the desert continues,
in the promised land of our abiding hammock
we are already home. 7/2/21

Perhaps nothing calls for courage more than empathy.

Where's This in the History Book?

Try for a second, White America,
to imagine the terror of traveling after sundown
without the Green Book.
Where's this in the history book
of the fabled land of the just,
the rumored home of the free? 7/4/21

Appalling the claim to be God's people. See where it leads.

"O but We are His People"

What kind of God
would promise milk and honey on the land of others
that His people would then have to displace
in order to fulfill His promise?
An invented God
to justify theft and murder. 7/4/21

Should not every people rightfully feel chosen?

Looking Every Elsewhere

Until every people is recognized as chosen,
every land revered as holy,
we will wander sad and parched in the desert
looking every elsewhere
for milk and honey flowing. 7/4/21

Let's not go overboard with independence, even on Independence Day.

Declaration of Dependence

While some today sing of independence,
may the single family sing of *de*pendence--
on warming sun,
vivifying air,
kinship with every living thing
on uniquely hospitable Earth. 7/4/21

Companionship, whether in sorrow or joy, is that not what we most hunger?

Never Alone

To call it a vale of tears,
this valley of darkness where we dwell,
simply reminds us when we weep
we weep not alone.
Neither are we alone
when standing on the summit of Mt. Existence
singing gratitude to the sun! 7/4/21

It has always made sense to me why Memory was the mother of the Muses.

Without Memory What Would We Have?

It's not just forgetting what I did moments prior,
it's looking at a face etched in memory
with the name totally escaping.
What sprang like a flash now takes its sweet time,
somewhere lingering till flash it's back.
Instead of decrying this evident slippage,
auguring perhaps the cliff's not-far off fall-off,
I am startled awake to the wonder
of the mother of the Muses named Memory.
Without her what would we have? 7/5/21

Robert Browning isn't lumped with the Romantics, but from the following he might have been.

Summum Bonum

"All the breath and the bloom of the year in the bag of one
bee,
all the wonder and wealth of the mine in the heart of one
gem,
in the core of one pearl all the shade and the shine of the
sea"--
Robert Browning was just getting started.
What a delight to see at the lyrical ending
where it was that this seeker had found
not only breath and bloom, wonder and wealth, shade and
shine
but the brightest truth and purest trust in all the universe--
"all were for me in the kiss of one girl." 7/6/21

That Browning wrote "Summum Bonum" when almost eighty was for me the icing on the cake. Years aren't a fright when a heart is right.

Octogenarian Rhapsody

More than a delight, a confirmation!
When Robert Browning rhapsodized
about the brightest truth and purest trust in all the universe
that he found in the kiss of one girl,
I leapt when I learned he was near eighty!
An octogenarian myself in but two months,
I smile to be reminded by a fellow romantic
that rhapsodizing need never be over
as long as the heart romps in clover. 7/19/21

*"Campaign of misinformation" has a modern ring but
a long history.*

Excruciating Crosswords

Travel back into the minds
of White Southerners despairing
as the Confederacy of their dreams
went up literally in smoke.
What an excruciating crossroads--
admit to an accusing world
the shame of your defense of an institution
at the heart of your rationale to secede
or try instead by changing the narrative
to redeem your pride at the expense of your shame.
Opting for the latter (can we not understand?)
they conjured the claim that slavery
was but the pretext for Northern aggression
against an agrarian culture envied,
that big government with overwhelming force
had ruthlessly stomped states' rights into the ground.
"America's second revolution" may have been thwarted,
so went the new creed,
but at root its cause was both valiant and noble--
to deny it is not only to wave the bloody shirt
but to play the race card!
Does not the question remain haunting --
can redemption worthy of the name
ever be achieved by burying shame? 7/7/21

It wasn't long before I found it, but I wish not to forget a realization arising before I did.

One of the Keenest of Love's Gifts

Unable to find my journal
having looked everywhere I can think,
I am seized by worry.
What if it were truly gone?
Seeing me carry it everywhere
my wife more than any in the world
would fathom my loss.
Which gets me realizing one of the keenest of love's gifts
lies in knowing there will always be someone
who fathoms the meaning of your loss.
Think of the sorrow compounding sorrow
were there no one. 7/8/21

That there are so many songs about love tells you something. Here's one more.

This Immortal Diamond We Call Love

I'll tell you how strong is love.
Wherever they go when they vanish
they take us with them,
and whenever we stand still and remember,
they're right here.
What words we still whisper
in the secret most chambers
of our forever-connected hearts.
Stronger than the world, I tell you,
this immortal diamond we call love. 7/9/21

A long prelude to "And a Little Child Will Lead Them." In the midst of putting photos in an album for Brewster's 6th birthday (1/26), Penny asked me to see if I could find things in my journal to provide some details. I sent her the following from my journal on 3/30/21: "James was transfixed while recounting Brewster's amazing relabeling his situation with all kinds of magic robots, super spacemen, and an army of helpers to defend him in the battle against the nukeemies, confident that he will prevail. Couldn't ask for a better attitude when facing a dark unknown." After reading it, Penny's face scrunched up (common to all editors) and said she had in mind more details. So I headed back to my journal and found the following, copied verbatim from this well fortified five-year-old an exact month later, 4/30/21: "The crane drops a net over the nukeemies and then the laser traps them while the ghosties who have pistols scare away the other nukeemies and then the giant tanks and rocket launchers and machine guns are all filled with cold cold medicine because the nukeemies don't like the cold...After the whole team cleans up all the bacteria there's a big feast to celebrate the victory—chicken and rice casserole, turkey and dressing with gravy, green beans and corn and burned boiled potatoes and bunches of food and then ice cream with double chocolate chips." I never did check how the potatoes got burned but that didn't seem to detract from the feast.

To Brewster's many well-wishers who have been holding him (along with his family) in the light, clearly in the mystery of things he has felt it. Glow to realize you are part of his squadron of defenders! A deeply grateful thank you from GG and Pop Pop and Brewster's other grandparents Siddy and Pops.
Keep it up, squadron!

Charlie

And a Little Child Will Lead Them

My grandson with his squadron of defenders
announces the Nukeemies are done,
the battle has been won!
O he'll grant they'll keep storming back,
but what's to fear
with his squadron of defenders near?
Ah, to feel so protected. 7/14/21

You should have seen his pride when he and GG finally cracked it!

A Glittering Secret Center

After a hundred blows from Brewster and GG
the geode finally cracked open
to reveal a glittering secret center.
Each of us can only imagine
our own glittering secret center,
but others who love us can see it! 7/15/21

> Pop Pop
> Lookout Mountain
> Tennessee
> United States
> North America
> Western hemisphere
> Planet Earth
> Solar System
> Milky Way Galaxy
> Universe. July 15, 2021

*And little did I know, until Brewster announced it on a visit to
Virginia, that Hicky was a she. Who am I to argue with a budding
Druid?*

Leafy Wizards Watching Over

Hicky and Hacky
seemed to Pop Pop and Brewster
just the right names for a hickory in Virginia
and a hackberry in Tennessee,
leafy wizards watching over them each. 7/17/21

*An illuminating moment from a workshop on the
Quaker Thomas Kelly.*

Mutterings

Invited to read pages of Thomas Kelly quotes
and then choose the one most striking,
I smiled at the futility since so many struck home
until one jumped from the crowd,
seized me by the collar,
and shouted, "This is it, buster!"
"Begin where you are. Obey now."
Always begin again, I muttered,
not appreciating being jostled.
And what's it supposed to mean anyway
being obedient to *now*?
Kelly's own muttering seemed to come from the wings,
"That's for you, dear obscure one,
to figure out." 7/21/21

It's easy to castigate until we look in the mirror.

Before Casting Any Stones

I find myself wondering
what if Trump experienced such a come to Jesus moment
that he fell on his knees weeping genuine tears
for choosing power over truth,
the acclaim of the few with the most
and to hell with the least?
I'll grant I'm not holding my breath,
but before casting any stones
I might acknowledge before God and conscience
(are the two not indistinguishable?)
my own less than scintillating track record with truth,
my own recurring disinclination
to pay more than lip-service to the least of these.
Might not every last one of us
have reason to fall on our knees
weeping genuine tears? 7/23/21

If the Divine is assumed to dwell in loftiness beyond feeling, how then call this Presence the epitome of love?

Musing on Affecting the Cosmic Heart

What if instead of something or someone "out there"
what we call God is the propulsion within every particle
to climb the mountain of the universe
toward greater consciousness the summit of which is love?
And if something akin to joy is stirred in God's heart
whenever we lend the weight of our own love to the climbing,
how not then something akin to sorrow
whenever we choose not to? 7/23/21

There's something about vigil candles in a darkened church.

Giving Witness

O to be a tiny candle in the darkened hush
of synagogue, church, or mosque
giving witness to a flaming Presence
that will never be able to be extinguished
by finger pinch or puff of air. 7/25/21

It does wonders for breath-appreciation to remember a final one is coming.

Breath

However many breaths remain
before they stop coming,
may we sink into amazement
before the absolute gratuity and sweetness
of the next one. 7/25/21

"Each mortal thing...crying What I do is me, for that I came" was how Hopkins sang of it.

Unique in the Whole Cosmic Sweep

Sui generis.
Its own genus and genius.
Constituting a class alone.
One of a kind.
Unique in the whole cosmic sweep.
"Each mortal thing"
includes that face in the mirror.
Let it sink in. 7/25/21

Incarnation is one of the big words, inviting reconsideration.

The Problem with the Incarnation

The only problem
but not an insignificant one
with the church's doctrine of the Incarnation
is that to bow before Matter becoming Spirit,
Flesh becoming Word,
implies Matter and Flesh were devoid to begin with
of the power of Spirit and the poetry of Word.
Why is it so hard to imagine
a casing of already-enfleshed seed
with the spirited dream of a flower? 7/25/21

Joseph Campbell's way of sounding an alarm was "Beware the error of the found truth."

The Truly Hoodwinked

Taken in.
Duped.
Hoodwinked.
How quick we are to hurl the word
at those on the far side of the chasm
only to hear them hurling to us back
the very same word!
Becoming less hoodwinked--
is that not at bottom what it's all about,
this journey of spirit
continuously searching inner as well as outer skies
for Truth's shooting star?
Are not the truly hoodwinked
the ones no longer searching? 7/26/21

Words can never nail down, but they can point. The quote at the bottom is from The Divine Milieu.

Teilhard Ran out of Words

Rather than running down,
the universe is building toward culmination,
consummation,
consecration,
communion.
Teilhard ran out of words
before the incandescence of a vision. 7/27/21

Teilhard's Vision

"The diaphany of the divine
at the heart of the universe
on fire!" 8/5/21

"Embrace your death," exclaimed Thomas Berry. "It will serve you."

Where Today Can I Plant a Seed?

Pondering the dying to come
of everything I hold dear,
my own life not excluded,
heightens for me the riveting realization
that I'm still here!
With tomorrow not guaranteed,
where today can I plant a seed? 7/28/21

Mindful of Michelangelo, here's a question to ponder at the beginning of a day.

What David Will Step Forth?

What David will step forth
from the malleable white marble
of this glistening new day? 7/28/21

Flaming words from William Butler Yeats might, who knows, re-ignite the flame of another.

There Was a Fire in My Head

"I went out to the hazel wood
Because a fire was in my head"--
hopefully each one reading
can remember such a moment
and by this remembering spark alive
an ember holding to hope
of combusting back to fire. 7/29/21

Dumbstruck--the most fitting response when contemplating the igniting of the cosmos. Be wary of either quick explanation or ho-hum evasion.

How Not be Struck Dumb?

Pondering the blast-off imponderable Big Bang,
don't we have to wonder who struck the match,
ignited the primeval propulsion?
BEHOLD THE GREATEST MYSTERY EVER--
how not be struck dumb? 7/29/21

I'm no longer a Jesuit but still feel the heat from Ignatius.

Heat-Waves Still Reach

Imagine the heat
in the heart of a crippled soldier
as he labored up a mountain
to find the shrine of his Lady
so he could lay at her feet
on the feast of her Annunciation
his sword and his life!
Heat-waves still reach
five hundred years after. 7/30/21

Allow memory to re-activate.

Remember the Jolt

What perfect reply
to the transfixing of lightning's wonder—
thunder!
May remembering the jolt
from the flash and the bolt
once lighting our way
call back to our hearts
grown tepid over time
the glory of the wonder
of our *own* once-bracing thunder. 7/30/21

Further thoughts on the feast day of Ignatius. The man left a mark.

Extending Incarnation

Not by chance did Ignatius
lay his sword at the feet of his Lady
nine exact months before the birth
we celebrate at Christmas.
Annunciation!
What armor of our own
is it time to lay down?
And what have we each
extending Incarnation
to announce to the world? 7/31/21

A prophet is not easy to have around.

Obsessive-Compulsive Nuts

St. Ignatius, it is now suggested,
was an obsessive-compulsive nut.
Remembering Moses, St. Paul, and George Fox,
can you think of a prophet who wasn't? 7/31/21

A cherished ritual.

Some Bonds You Just Know

Each afternoon at 3
Brewster and Pop Pop face-time
whether for story-reading or just chatting.
Some bonds you just know will last forever. 7/31/21

Anniversaries of loved ones departed provide occasions for new understandings.

Felicitous Realization

Pondering my various spirit grandmothers
on this day when Cathy crossed the Rainbow Bridge
brings home the felicitous realization:
my sister now is one of my grandmothers! 8/1/21

A marriage to the end for us all.

Till Death Do Us Part

Imagining this coming month
all who will draw their first breath
and this coming month
all who will breathe their last
calls back the marriage till death do us part
of joy and sorrow in each human heart. 8/1/21

Can seizure of another's land be just, even if deemed divinely promised?

Always an Annihilating Ambition

It's as ironic as it is tragic
that oppressed brutally for millennia not just centuries
Jews have become in modern day Israel
the brutal oppressors.
Always an annihilating ambition--
to seize land divinely promised.
For any standing in the way,
 well, that's their problem. 8/2/21

*Bowing to mystery, then rising to kindness—now that's what
I call worship.*

Would That We Bowed More in Awe

The existence of God,
voice of God.
designs of God,
love of God.
wrath of God.
heart of God.
death of God.
face of God.
Let's just say humankind
gives this Force animating all that is
called by whatever or no name
a lot of attention.
Great Mystery and Presence
for me come closest.
Would that we argued less
about the name of the Who
or the nature of the What
and bowed more in awe to Great Mystery
calling us to kindness.   8/3/21

If God is complete, what are we here for?

What Dignity to be Invited

What if the Vision Quest of the universe
were God's ever expansion?
What dignity to be invited
to enhance the great Dance! 8/3/21

*Dogmas must somehow touch on truth. Dismissing them leaves us
diminished.*

Trinitarian Conjecture

Ignition, fuel, oxygen--
striking a match to light incense this morning
brought home in a flash
why those hoping to throwing light
on a universe blazing out of night
deemed essential all three. 8/3/21

Astounding the complexity of us each.

God Only Knows

Each of us
is so singular and complex
that Great Mystery alone
not only comprehends but cherishes
our story for the ages. 8/6/21

I'll admit it begins awkward, conversing with another who is masked, but think to what it calls attention.

Masked Opportunities

Not being able to see the face
(except for the eyes)
of the person with whom you're talking
forces focus on twin amazements.
Undistracted by moving lips,
don't you have to lean to catch
each stunningly distinct voice?
And when it comes to surprise,
when have you paid such attention
to the riveting revelation of eyes? 8/8/21

I'm big on anniversaries, especially ones marking decisions at forks in the road, each making all the difference.

"All We Want is for You to be Happy"

Some days stand out, shout REMEMBER.
62 years ago today
I bid adieu to tearful mother and bewildered father
when entering the Society of Jesus.
Ten exact years later
I upended both again (having gotten used to the idea)
by *leaving* the Society of Jesus.
As if they needed more consternation,
soon thereafter I not only left the church
but after nomadic years searching
landed eventually with the Quakers!
Be aware when telling your children
that all you want is their happiness--
their notion of happiness just might turn out
not to be in accord with your own.
Consternation aside,
be happy if later they tell you they found
what you long ago wished them. 8/8/21

Think how many of your wisdom figures had no biological children.
Hear their blessing from the wings— thanks to you they are
emphatically not childless!

No They Did Not!

Ecstatic realization
when reflecting on spirit-titans in my life--
Loren Eiseley being just one, Mary Oliver another--
who assumed they died childless.
No they did not! 8/7/21

A new way to sing of his vision: Matter is embryonic Spirit!

The Way Teilhard Saw It

The way Teilhard saw it
Spirit did not by supernatural touch
call lowly matter to life,
rather Matter was Spirit dreaming from the beginning
of bursting into flower—
and the full flower is not yet! 8/10/21

I remember struggling in high school to comprehend the meaning of metaphor. What a journey bearing fruit it's been since.

From the Literal to the Metaphoric

That two writers growing up Protestant,
Carl Jung and Sue Monk Kidd,
could sing praise for Mary's assumption into heaven
celebrated on this day by Catholics
hints at the reality of the radiance and the reach
of a myth that can live.
Feast on the possibility
that the journey from the literal to the metaphoric
instead of marking lamentable loss
speaks actually of luminous leap. 8/15/21

Anniversaries can be light or dark, sometimes both on the same day.

Depending Where We Place Attention

On this day years past
yes was the response to a momentous question
paving the way for a long bright journey.
On this day years later
a loved one took his life
ending a dark shorter journey.
Depending where we place attention
we smile or we weep. 8/18/21

It beggars the mind, wondering my own response in a calamity such as one of these.

Assaults Human and Natural

Afghanistan and Haiti--
such fear and trembling in the wake of assault
whether the assault be human or natural.
May those caught in the crush of calamity
somehow find comfort, somehow find courage
when consumed with fear and trembling
the rest of us scarcely can conceive. 8/18/21

My search to understand "transformation" will continue, but this marks a realization along the way.

Transformation Enough for Me

I've long shied from "praying for transformation"
presuming being transformed meant being transported
to some lofty region beyond fear.
Long acquainted from early childhood
with fears embedded to the point of instinctive,
I know better.
But even embedded fears diminish
when I remember whose I am,
find courage when there was none.
Transformation enough for me. 8/22/21

A question to ask at the start of a day.

When My Head Hits the Pillow

What if each morning upon rising
you put to yourself this question?
What is the one thing--
when my head this evening hits the pillow--
the one task of all those facing me
that I want to look back on and say,
I did that well today!
The one ball important to keep in the air
regardless how many others fell.
The one word needing to be spoken
that I spoke.
The one encounter in the general rush
to which I was fully present
and my presence made a difference.
The one thing I can smile to look back upon
when my head this evening hits the pillow. 8/24/21

Not to be forgotten from a day in DC.

Riveting Hands

Left hand,
fingers furled in a fist;
right hand,
fingers relaxed and open.
Something about those two hands
captures the essence of the man
whose memory is enshrined forever
in the hush of his temple.
I was riveted yet again
in the National Gallery hours later
before Rodin's Hand of God.
Human and divine,
hands held me that day. 8/25/21

It's easier and quicker to peck out a letter on the keyboard, then hit "send" and be done. Ah, but not as sweetly done as it might have been, especially for an important one.

Written by Hand

Go find one,
a letter saved over the years
from one dear to your heart--
likely gone now but not gone
thanks to written words still pulsing
on a page you can *feel*.
After that makes your day,
make someone else's
looking back some distant day
on words of your own still pulsing.
Before pecking at the keyboard,
remember how you felt when reading
a letter to you written by hand. 8/25/21

The simple things are the most profound.

Gargantuan Pleasure

For a fact it is coming,
the day when one last time
my lungs will breathe out
and not breathe back in.
Depressing to contemplate,
is that what you think?
If so you're missing the gargantuan pleasure
I experience when aware with a rush of thanksgiving
I still have the unspeakable luxury
of breathing back in! 8/26/21

East—does not the very word brighten?

Bowing to the East

Just think, no day following night
were Spaceship Earth, with us aboard,
not spinning endlessly to the East,
turning magically each morning
black sky into blue feast.
How our ancestors must be cheering
when we join them in bowing
with our Mother to the East. 8/26/21

If terrifying to view from afar, what to have been there?

O My God

Kabul airport., August 2021.
Desperation rising to panic.
Leaving literally everything behind
if lucky enough to make it with loved ones
on one of the last flights.
If not, o my god what then?
Call it life under the Taliban
with ISIS planning detonations
to take us to kingdom come?
That man jostling behind us,
o my god, he has a backpack! 8/27/21

Catastrophe in Kabul --
black ink flows red
across shuddering page. 8/27/21

For an entire political party to get on board of transparent deception speaks of desperation for political survival—so what if the collateral damage is democracy.

Please, No Whining about the Constitution

Let's make it harder to vote
for those less likely to vote
for our guys.
Please, no whining about the Constitution
when at stake is our political survival. 8/28/21

I'd like to believe it sent a tremble.

Steer Clear of Our Gardens!

Three deer in the woods
are munching their way
toward me sitting here quietly
with the newly risen sun
generously spreading light over us all.
Munch away, gentle ones,
just steer clear, if you know what is good for you,
of our gardens! 8/28/21

As it is hard for the individual, perhaps it's even harder for the nation—stepping back to see what is.

Wondering about the Culture of America

What is it about the culture of America
quick to cheer war,
question the patriotism
of any protesting war,
shun accountability
for the wreckage that follows war?
Do you ever wonder? 8/29/21

Hard to imagine which is worse, living smack in the path of a hurricane or a war.

Must Feel Something like War

Yet another hurricane bears down
on the coast of Louisiana
sixteen years to the devastating day
when New Orleans was inundated by Katrina.
I'm trying to imagine the terror
of having to flee for our lives
not knowing when or if we'd return
and what there'd be to return to.
Must feel something like war. 8/29/21

Deep listen to a peacemaker, and feel fire from a furnace.

Waging Peace

To hear one speak who has walked the peace walk--
paying a price few can fathom,
feeling a world-tenderness few can fathom--
gives a glimpse into the manner of soldiering
alone that can win peace.
"Blessed are the peacemakers," it has been said,
for they will be called children of God." 9/1/21

Let's just say a phrase from the long ago catechism caught my attention this day.

Double Blinding

Blinding, we are told it will be,
the beatific face-to-face vision.
Blinded we already are
if we miss God in the next face. 8/29/21

Beatific vision--
mystics keep reminding
we don't have to wait. 8/29/21

A handshake never to be forgotten.

Holy Days

33 years ago last evening
my father shook my hand
before a coma overtook him.
33 years ago this morning
he crossed over the last bridge.
Churches understand the importance
of holy days.   9/1/21

Handshake always firm,
his final was the firmest.
Words were not needed.   8/31/21

*This will resonate with those recognizing the ancient foe we
have in common.*

Be Suspicious of Spiritual Airs

My instinct when asked to do something
is to feel put upon.
Poor me I had things planned
that now have to wait.
Another buried instinct is to please,
rather not to displease,
meaning I'm quick to impress others
with my readiness to help
lest I come down in their estimation.
After nearly eighty years
of being praised for my altruism,
I smile a wry smile
long acquainted with instincts buried
carried by my race across millions of years.
Which doesn't mean they can't be controlled
and ever so slowly diminished
(else what meaning the moral life?),
it's just a reminder that any achievement of altruism
is a repeated choice against an ancient foe.
Be suspicious of spiritual airs
claiming the foe is defeated. 8/30/31

Some things you remember long after.

With the Force of Revelation

Things crystallize in a moment,
in time beyond time--
kairos, not chronos.
37 exact years ago
it came with the force of revelation:
"Here, can you find me here,
can you love me here?"
A moment in time
glimpsing the possibility hidden
in *every* moment in time. 8/30/21

Think of the tale wolves could tell about humans.

Hoping Humans Might Creep in to Listen

A friend sent me Thomas Peacock's *The Wolf's Trail*
trusting I would move in close to listen --
Ojibwe wisdom by way of a story
from wolf uncle to wolf pups around a fire
hoping humans from the surrounding dark and cold
might creep in to listen. 8/30/21

It's hard to pick just one.

My Special Times

My special times are early morning
with sun rising in hope before me,
early evening
with sun setting in gratitude behind me,
deep night when I sink back into mystery
trusting moon and stars to watch over
before sun rises in hope the next morning. 9/3/21

Long ago I struggled with the meaning of metaphor. Now I'm electrified to understand.

If You Can Hold to the Metaphoric

The literal is awesome:
It really happened!
The metaphoric is beyond awesome:
It's *still* happening!
The whole sweep of time
if you can hold to the metaphoric
is NOW in the temple of imagination. 9/5/21

It was exactly 37 years ago, and I'm still there on the edge of my seat.

Witnessing John Muir Back Alive!

Many years ago in Yosemite
I witnessed suddenly back alive
no less phenomenon than John Muir!
Storyteller and actor Lee Stetson
invited us to the edge of our seats
to eavesdrop on conversations with a tramp.
Next evening I returned to be transfixed once more.
Ah, words, though they ever fail
to catch the full wind in the sail,
nevertheless can open up sky
into which open hearts can fly! 9/5/21

You tell me, if your heart is beyond being affected, how in blazes can you set foot in love's temple?

Can Love be Unmoved?

Imagining a swelling in God's heart
upon receiving from a human heart love
evokes cries of blasphemy from dogmatists
insisting Deity by definition can't change.
What possibly could it mean then,
their incongruous claim God is love?
Can love be unmoved? 9/5/21

A visit from a friend of the heart is always a very big deal.

Leaning on Every Moment

When a friend of the heart comes to visit
whose age and infirmity make future visits iffy,
how not lean on every moment
to maximize the cherishing.
But then isn't this always the case
regardless age or infirmity
when a friend of the heart comes to visit? 9/6/21

*Chesterton once said that to appreciate something, imagine it lost.
The same holds true for a friend, particularly if possibly near
his end.*

The Gift of His Longer Living

Seeing a photo of himself years ago
he was struck that even then he appeared gaunt
wondering if perhaps it was then
that the cancer was beginning.
His countless friends marvel
at the gift of his longer living
they graciously have been given. 9/9/21

Let's just say Oh and Ah are ever at it.

The Dance Goes On

Mouse: Oh no, what should I say?
What if it flops, what will they think of me?
Moose: Ah, an opportunity to give voice,
what only matters is what I think of me!
And the mousemoose dance goes on. 9/8/21

There aren't enough songs for evolution.

Luminous March Forward

Think of evolution
whether personal or cosmic
as less discarding the useless than incorporating the useful
in the luminous march forward
toward spellbinding flowering
hidden in each living seed. 9/8/21

Morality trumps theology any day.

Before You Pity or Applaud

Before you pity unbelievers in God,
look to the quality of their love
for their neighbor and the living planet.
Before you applaud believers in God,
look to the quality of their love
for their neighbor and the living planet.
Is that not what God must look to
if there is one? 9/10/21

Read about so-called Reconstruction and cry.

The True Lost Cause

If you pause to wonder
how America's approximation of apartheid
called segregation
held on after slavery was ended
by bloody war and constitutional amendment,
look no further than the mighty effort--
for more than a century successful
and still alive and ill in the minds of many--
to defeat the nobility of the true lost cause
ruefully called Reconstruction. 9/10/21

9/11's tragedy doesn't compare with what we used it to justify.

How Not Weep?

How not weep
looking back twenty years
to remember not only burning towers
but the squandering of America's national treasury
(not to mention her reputation in the world)
by arrogance and deceit,
thirst for vengeance,
and the withering wreckage of two nations
all out of the toxic combination
of wounded ego and oil greed? 9/11/21

I'll wager I'm not the only one glowing to remember Malcolm Miller,
guide for decadess at Chartres.

Rapt Both Then and in the Remembering

I hear him still
expounding to the rapt cluster of us
of the Blue Virgin,
John the Baptist on the facade,
stained windows rising skyward
hallowing the hush of the darkness within,
labyrinth at the center
over a well honoring the Goddess
before the torch was passed to Mary.
Here I am 43 years later
in the hush of my own green cathedral
rapt as Sun's rising through Gothic trees
begins staining dark sky virgin blue! 9/12/21

*"Except for the point, the still point, there would be no dance,
and there is only the Dance." These words from T. S. Eliot's Four
Quartets get to the core?*

To the Music of the Only Dance

Sun and shadow,
masculine and feminine,
action and contemplation,
making be and letting be,
giving voice and remaining silent--
rather than opposites
much less enemies contending
see these as partners swaying in and out
to the music of the only Dance. 9/12/21

Imagine Teilhard's eyes as he sang of it.

"You"

While nothing says it all
given Great Mystery behind, within, and ahead,
perhaps "You" comes closest.
Christianity's flaws notwithstanding,
is not the essence of its announcement,
wild pronouncement,
that at the heart of Great Mystery
luring the universe toward wider compassion
is a "You"?
Think what it must have been
to watch Teilhard's eyes as he sang of it--
behind, within, ahead of a universe still birthing,
You! 9/15/21

How naïve to think a couple years back that the biological and political plagues assailing us soon would be gone.

Plagues Can Return with a Vengeance

Somehow I got on the mailing list
of Team Trump calling upon "patriots"
to shell out more in the righteous cause
of the return of the Still President.
Plagues, as we are sadly learning,
can not only hang on
but return with a vengeance
if we have failed in sufficient numbers
to inoculate ourselves. 9/13/21

This will speak to any of the fortunate ones to have been expanded by the wisdom, and inspired by the courage, of John Shelby Spong.

September 12th has Become Holy

September 12th has become holy
for marking the day when a man intoxicated with God
crossed the bridge into Great Mystery.
May the tower of his wisdom,
power of his presence,
shower of his blessings
never be forgotten by those indeed blessed
by Jack Spong crossing their path. 9/15/21

They were coming from afar to be with me on my 80th. Imagine my anticipatory joy.

Forged by the Fire of Long Friendship

I beam to await
in a circle of stones in a tree cathedral
the arrival of two friends
coming to honor and deepen a bond
forged decades ago in Chicago.
How can the Cosmic Conspirator
not be smiling at the reconvening at Cor Mundi
of three forged by the fire of long friendship? 9/15/21

I only pretended to take umbrage.

Reprieve from a White Tornado

My wife doesn't obsess so much
when the guests coming are all male.
"They either won't notice the details
or won't care."
I feign offense at the slight to my gender
smiling to have a reprieve from the need
for a comprehensive white tornado. 9/16/21

What would be on your flag?

If Your Body Became a Flag

Not many I hang with sport tattoos
(at least not that you can see)
but what a fertile heart trip to take
imagining what and where it would be
if today was the day your body became a flag
waving an announcement to the world! 9/22/21

Children are mystics until they are taught the straight and narrow.

Let Your Inner Mystic out to Play

I deem it a worthy cause
to bring mysticism down from the clouds
lest folks keep thinking it's far out of reach.
Become like the little children, wise ones say,
let your inner mystic out to play. 9/25/21

If, according to Kazantzakis, the best definition of God is Ah!, you'd think cosmologists would be the most religious. Perhaps, sans creed, they are.

Think Galaxies and be Blown Away

Think galaxies and be blown away,
more numerous, Carl Sagan claimed,
than grains of sand on all Earth beaches!
Surely he exaggerates I think
trying to compute in order to refute.
Don't be such a jerk, over rational C.
Just call it a soulful skyful
and let yourself be blown way! 9/26/21

Common expressions often contain gold.

It Struck Me

Next time when saying "it struck me,"
stop and bow down before the wonder
that something just flashed across your sky
exploding from your heart thunder! 9/26/21

Listen to a thousand insomniacs and toss and turn with a thousand tales.

Until Empathy Comes to the Rescue

Having a hard time sleeping sometimes
triggers woe is me
until empathy comes to the rescue
reminding me countless elsewhere unsleeping
have worries dwarfing my own.
Minor inconvenience
doesn't come close to genuine worry. 9/27/21

Insomnia can lead
to self-pity or compassion.
It's a choice. 9/27/21

A guideline to remember when discussing religion.

Kindness is the Only Way

Is there one God or many
or no God at all,
and which religion holds the Truth
if there is such?
Let there be no arguing
about what can never be settled
at the level of the head.
How do we of the single family
then open the heart-door
so respectful listening holds sway?
Kindness, sisters and brothers,
kindness is the only way. 9/28/21

Those graced by animals have a wider family.

Kinship across Species

Today was hard for our puppy.
Unforeseen reactions to shots
led to more shots hours later
until finally pain and lethargy lifted.
Though brief as crises go,
it served to remind us of kinship across species--
suffering's central place,
comforting's abiding grace. 10/14/21

However you start the morning, be grateful you have another to start.

My Tried and True Way

Imagining myself on my deathbed
is my tried and true way
to begin opening the glittering present
of the gift of another day. 10/18/21

Imagine Just One No Longer Breathing

On particularly disgruntled mornings
when bemoaning minimal sleep,
bodily complaints
and worries swarming,
when, in other words, things are peachy ripe
for self-pity to have a field day,
it helps to imagine just one
of the billions no longer breathing
yearning to cross back over the bridge
for the gigantic pleasure of a breath again,
of the chance to lift another's heart again
at the start of a breathgiving new day. 10/26/21

What awesome organ in the human breast, this flowering of evolution called the heart.

Deeper Than the Deep Blue Sea

Too much beauty
the heart nearly bursts,
too much suffering
the heart nearly breaks.
Softer than down,
stronger than steel,
deeper than the deep blue sea,
the heart in you and me. 10/21/21

I trust Gerard Manley Hopkins will not mind his "shining like shook foil" employed in the honoring of a fellow Jesuit.

Feel the Flame

"The diaphany"
(light rising up, shining through)
"of the divine"
(called by a thousand names,
beyond naming)
"at the heart"
(flaming out from the very core
like shining from shook foil)
"of the universe"
(the One Great Turning catching everything up
in its gravitational wild embrace)
"on fire."
(think of it,
at the heart of it all
not excluding the face in the mirror,
FIRE.)
Feel the flame from Teilhard's vision
caught in his incandescent single phrase:
"The diaphany of the divine at the heart of the universe
on fire." 10/28/21

We don't need Shakespeare for drama.

I Can't Wait to Find Out

What mark will this day make on me?
What mark will I make on this day?
I can't wait till this evening
to look back and find out.
What drama today! 10/29/21

How can I not sing of Joseph Campbell?

Gone Only if We Forget Him

On this day in 1987
Joseph Campbell breathed his last--
a Gandalf calling Bilbos and Frodos
on brave adventures to the Mt. of Doom
to save nothing less than the world;
an Arthur exhorting his knights
to enter the forest at its darkest
on the golden trail of the Grail;
a scholar whose library was his church
with holy stories of thousand-faced heroes
divining God beneath every mask.
He's left if we let him,
is gone only if we forget him. 10/30/21

Todos Los Santos.

Continuing Presence of the Seeming Departed

⌣⌐

Tonight is All Hallow's Eve.
I'd not make Halloween less festive--
what masked fun to go incognito!--
just remind what it's all about:
preparation for celebration, not mourning,
on the Day of the Dead tomorrow.
All Saints Day used to feel anti-climatic
following the excitement of the evening before,
not to mention heavy with solemnity
remembering all those here no longer.
But thanks to Todos Los Santos
Halloween becomes a literal dress rehearsal
for tomorrow's hallowed Day of Remembrance
of the continuing presence of the seeming departed
in the heaven of our hearts. 10/31/21

If exercise is vital for keeping our body in shape, what about the shape of our soul?

Most Necessary of Spirit Muscles

⌣⌐

Since courage is called for not once
but time after time after time again--
like a thousand times daily!--
one had better have a daily spirit practice
strengthening that most necessary of spirit muscles
called courage. 11/1/21

After our silence under the trees, a story had to be shared.
It made our day.

I'm on the Moon!

⤳

"Before we go I have to tell you
about my transformative experience this morning."
A young boy at swim class at the Y
had been terrified of going into the water,
even where it was shallow.
Multiple coaxings had failed
until an imaginative coach with a tendering touch
(narrator of this recounting)
suggested they go in together where it was shallow
with their little fingers linked.
""I'm on the moon!"
was all an elated little boy could later utter
when looking back to realize he had done it!
"I'm on the moon!" the narrator now uttered,
having witnessed the transformation.
"I'm on the moon!" my heart leapt to agree
pondering the power and the beauty
of empathy mingling with imagination
to coax courage from a frightened little boy
by interlocking little fingers!   11/1/21

Mementos from early November mornings.

Waiting to Astonish

It slows you down
to wake you up
to a corner of creation
waiting to astonish.
A poem. 11/2/21

Nuggets for the Journey

"Start where you are. Obey now."
Nuggets from Thomas Kelly
to carry one on the journey
to a kingdom at hand. 11/3/21

At Just the Right Angle

Dew-diamonds spied
at just the right angle
reveal jewels of every-hue!
Might it not be the same
for each of our moments spied
at just the right angle? 11/3/21

Joseph Campbell called it aesthetic arrest. The Greeks claimed it's when chronos becomes kairos. I call it a touch of glory.

When the Chronological Clock Stood Still

When the heart is arrested the clock stands still.
43 years may have passed
since I was spellbound in the Uffizi
before Botticelli's Birth of Venus and Primavera,
but I need only close my eyes to be back there
when the chronological clock stood still. 11/4/21

Suddenly a piercing sorrow.

Wondering in Sorrow

Our side yard magnolia
blocked from the sun by tall oaks
in forty years has not flowered.
It gets me wondering in sorrow
what happens to magnolia human hearts
growing up deprived of love's sun? 11/4/21

Nothing has been the same since watching on the winter solstice a video of the sun's penetration into the heart of darkness.

Piercing, Impregnating Light

The penetration of a shaft of light at sunrise
into the absolute darkness of a tomb
in fact a womb
on the winter solstice at Newgrange in Ireland--
for some a dagger piercing
to the heart of night with redemptive light,
for others a passionate thrust
of advancing Sun to inaugurate life.
Falling shaft, rising shaft,
what symbol could be more suggestive
than piercing, impregnating light? 11/5/21

D. H. Lawrence might well have had Whitman in mind when writing "Be Building Your Ship of Death."*

Take Note as You are Building Your Vessel

A kelson is the backbone of a ship,
a longitudinal beam fastened to the keel
"to stiffen and strengthen."
No wonder Whitman's cry from *Leaves of Grass*:
"a kelson of creation is love!"
Take note as you are building your vessel
to cross the last sea. 11/6/21

**"Oh, build your ship of death, be building it now
With dim, calm thoughts and quiet hands
Putting its timbers together in the dusk,

Rigging its mast with the silent, invisible sail
That will spread in death to the breeze
Of the kindness of the cosmos, that will waft
The little ship with its soul to the wonder-goal."*

Savor Theresa's message. You not only have an interior castle,
it's made of diamonds!

A Castle Made of Diamonds

"I began to think of the soul
as a castle made of diamonds
in which there are many rooms,
a paradise in which God takes delight...
and in the very center of all
the principal one where takes place
the most secret intercourse between God and the soul."
Even if we knew no more than the title
of St. Theresa's *The Interior Castle,*
we'd be profoundly in her debt
for the reminder we each have one! 11/7/21

I'll not deny aggravation comes with a puppy, but so does unending
amusement (not to mention endearing affection).

Alternating Stillness with Play

"Be playful
and know that I am God."
A puppy in your lap
when you're trying to be still--
when pen attempting to write
becomes a moving target for a pounce--
must be amusing to God
as present in play as in stillness.
How rich a life alternating stillness with play,
abiding Presence blessing each. 11/9/21

It's hard to imagine before you get there.

Am I Speaking of This Day or My Life?

There's still light but it's fading,
trailing the fire of the day.
Am I speaking of this day or my life?
I think of myself at 80
as having begun a final fling
across autumn's cross-over into winter.
Hoping for a long slow decline
with woodstove warming and snow-beauty falling,
I'm not without recognition
that at any time on the door of my heart
can come a knock bidding me enter
death's mysterious dark cottage.
This is where the mind of one aging
goes when dusk begins engaging? 11/9/21

Dare to write a letter to a wisdom figure. It's been known to open a door.

A Flowering before a Fire

Some dates I soar to remember
like November 10, 1991--
before a fire with John Yungblut
exchanging epiphanies from our respective journeys,
discovering affinities running deep.
Reading, having sown the seed,
was nurtured by letter exchanges
which then led to a flowering before a fire
that has continued to nurture the soul
of this sojourner ever since. 11/10/21

"Ho-hum, just another day." You've got to be kidding.

What They Would Give to Have One More?

Dawn, spring;
noon, summer;
dusk, fall;
midnight, winter--
to think the whole span of a year
reenacted each day!
What all who have crossed over
would give to have one more. 11/12/21

There's often a poem waiting, even when it seems there isn't.

Irresistible Lure of a Pen

This morning my usually frisky puppy
loving to attack the moving target of my pen
is blissfully zonked out beside me.
Poised now with pen unassaulted,
nothing, wouldn't you know it, is coming
except the irresistible lure of a pen
for both puppy and poet. 11/12/21

In the warp and woof of things, death is an essential player. We
might wish it were otherwise until we try imagining it otherwise.

Can My Heart Roll out the Carpet?

If hibiscus buds are to open
thousands of aphids have to perish.
Ah, even with beauty comes sadness.
Can my heart following God's
roll out the carpet for both? 11/13/21

For adventure, we have only to wake in the morning.

Drama Rides Today on Each Wave

When I avoid challenge I jeer me,
when I embrace challenge I cheer me.
Drama rides on the wave
of each and every challenge
that will rock my boat today. 11/13/21

Playing with numbers.

With Old Age in Mind

Imagine 9 puffed up with promise,
poised on the brink of 1 joining up
once again with the infinity of 0. 11/15/21

Our Life as an 8

Think of the solstice point
where swirling pen meets in the center
of revolving joy/sorrow spheres
in the endless circledance. 11/15/21

Looking back on a fateful decision.

Forty-Six Years Later

I went back from the party to my place
inspired to *create something.*
Having heard Kevin sing and Ken recite his poem,
what have I to sing about, I wondered,
what in me yearns to be written?
Penny being white-hot on my mind--
this girl whose sudden reappearance
had dazzled me back into dreaming--
why not pour out what I feel in a letter?
Likely I'll never send it, I mused,
for exposing way too much of my heart.
Wouldn't you know it I then couldn't sleep
niggled by yet another inspiration.
Why *not* send it, dummy?
Who knows it just might persuade her
to reconsider before saying no
to my invitation to a date.
Moral of story?
Best not ignore an inspiration
that just possibly could change your life.
I didn't and it did. 11/16/21

About that letter.

Two Wonders I Could Scarcely Believe

Having just mailed the letter
on a long ago Sunday in Chicago
assuming it would get to the south side
Tuesday at the very earliest,
the last thing I wanted to receive
was a call from her on Monday
saying "I've thought it all over and the answer is no."
Oh no I thought
hearing the phone ring Monday evening,
let it not be her
before she's had a chance to see the letter!
Two wonders I could scarcely believe:
the letter had already reached her
and her answer was yes!
A complaint from me you will never hear
about the mail service in Chicago. 11/17/21

Just when things seemed progressing.

Days of Fury

Immune system being compromised
after each chemo assault
means potential invasion of new infection--
Brewster's fever hiking to 103
flashed high alert and danger.
These are the days of fury
within the body of a little boy
and the minds and hearts of loved ones hovering,
dealing with a darkness they never dreamed. 11/18/21

Some evenings the nightly news is unbearable

I Had To Look Away

"Senseless tragedy"--
we skip past the words
until they seize us by the collar
shouting "You must not look away!"
An SUV yesterday in Wisconsin
plowed into Thanksgiving parade bystanders
killing and maiming a score.
Despite the fists to my collar,
I had to look away.
My God,
members of a Dancing Grannies club
cheering schoolgirls strutting in bright colors
making music to remind us
regardless what happens
to never stop giving thanks.
We will betray them if we do. 11/22/21

"Row, row, row your boat"—hear the insistence if life is ever to reach the dream!

Are You Rowing, Sisters and Brothers?

Think of "justice for all"--
tacked onto the Pledge to declare our loftiest aspiration--
as a landing far upstream
only to be progressively attained
by strenuous paddling *against* the stream
of conviction baked into America's psyche
that power and privilege by tradition belong
to ones of white skin color.
Are you rowing, sisters and brothers, with all that is in you
toward that still-distant lofty aspiration
or letting the swift current of centuries
carry you unmerrily unmerrily unmerrily
further down that unrighteous stream? 11/28/21

Is it really unimaginable?

Troublesome Queries Sparked by James Michener

"It would be easy, if the United States turned sour,
to establish Nazi-like concentration camps
in almost any part of our nation
and find eager recruits to staff them."
What would the signs be, I wonder,
should our nation be turning sour?
Is it really unimaginable
as rhetoric inflames, divisions deepen, guns abound
that eager recruits would line up to staff
camps of darkness in a city once deemed
beacon on democracy's hill? 11/29/21

Beware when conscience is silenced by obedience.

Altars of Blind Obedience

"Blind obedience"--
the phrase came back last evening
while listening to one recount his experiences in the
military.
My own homage to blind obedience
took place in a seminary instead.
What happens to conscience
laid at the altar of blind obedience? 12/2/21

One can only hope.

Hopefully a Titanic Struggle

What hopefully is happening in the conscience
of one truly valuing honor
 at the same time supporting a politician
 who is the epitome of *dis*honor?
A titanic struggle. 12/2/21

Honor was clearly the theme of the day.

Honor--Jettison or Refurbish?

That so many give lip-service to honor
while supporting leaders embodying its opposite
makes one want either to jettison the word
or refurbish its radical radiance
with a nod toward Buddha and Jesus.
Make no mistake, regardless the cost
the truly religious pay homage to conscience. 12/2/21

Do not notions of cosmic alienation miss the universal matrix?

Fluke or Flowering?

Does humanity stand out like a sore thumb--
fluke conscious shoot
on the mindless stick of a universe--
or could each human simply be a flowering
of what the primordial living root
has been love-dreaming all along? 12/3/21

Pondering the power of small gestures.

Follow the Pain of Your Estrangement

"Estranged" is more painful than "stranger"
for ice now covers
hearts that were once warm.
But have not small gestures
been known to initiate thaws?
Follow the pain of your estrangement,
search for a small gesture. 12/5/21

I hear him still.

How Could I Forget?

"God is full of feeling!"--
so rang out a priest in a homily
near half a century ago.
If you ask me why I remember,
I answer how could I forget? 12/6/21

Always on Sacred Ground

"Feelings are sacramental,"
declared same priest the following day.
Sacramental points to sacred ground,
but feelings?
Were it true would we not
thanks to feelings daily in the thousands
be always on sacred ground? 12/7/21

A momentous crossing-over.

Crossing into Winter

Enamored all my life of the seasons,
I take particular note
when crossing the threshold into a new one.
Eight years ago today,
for reasons beyond doubting (some things you just know)
I felt in the core of the soul of me
I had crossed over into my winter.
There is so much more than meets the eye
in the rigorous vast kindness called winter. 12/7/21

*Preposterous, indeed blasphemous, to the orthodox is the suggestion
that Great Mystery (a.k.a. God) might also be in the dark about the
future, which is another reason I am deeply grateful to be unchained
from the orthodox.*

As Long as We Hold to the Path of Our Longing

What if even Great Mystery doesn't know
any more than you or I
when and how it will happen,
the exact circumstance of our final expiration?
Does it really matter
as long as we hold to the path of our longing,
savoring with bated breath what breathing remains?
Think the suspense if even Great Mystery wonders
not only the when but the how we will greet it,
that final expiration.
Of this we can absolutely be assured:
Great Mystery will be with us to meet it. 12/8/21

No attempt here to beguile from sorrow--necessary partner in the joysorrow dance--but to remind that what we lose we now carry within.

One More Has Taken up Residence

When yet another of the attachments of your heart
has disappeared from sight,
find solace in the midst of your sorrow
trusting that what it means is one more
has taken up permanent residence
in your heart's vast inner chamber
to both comfort and strengthen you
this day and every tomorrow. 12/8/21

Dogmas unable to stack up to reason can either be discarded with a good riddance or elevated to the high country of myth.

Celebrate Yourself along with Mary

Could there be a more dispiriting teaching
than "conceived in sin"
doubtless conceived in the desert
by a self-flagellating celibate?
On this feast of the Immaculate Conception,
celebrate yourself along with Mary--
lift dogma higher. 12/8/21

Empathy comes at a price.

Then Comes Empathy's Piercing

Before a woodstove fire as sky begins to brighten--
can you imagine a better way
to start the magnificence of a day?
Ah, but then comes empathy's piercing.
How would I be starting this day
(and what must have been last night?)
had I no home in which to retire
and at best a wistful longing
for a woodstove fire? 12/9/21

*This gives pleasure if for no other reason than conjoining the names
of Mary Oliver and Gerard Manley Hopkins.*

Rapture Binding Two Hearts

Wild with joy is my heart this morning
remembering "Hurrahing in Harvest" was the poem
Mary Oliver chose to end her essay on Hopkins.
His love-cry at the end gives a hint of the rapture
binding the hearts of them both.
"These things, these things were here and but the beholder
Wanting; which two when they once meet,
The heart rears wings bold and bolder
And hurls for him, O half hurls earth for him off under his
feet." 12/10/21

How many catastrophes will it take to shake us awake?

Stewardship's Abdication

Thinking of tornado-flattened Mayfield Kentucky
(but the most recent of rising natural disasters),
what if it's our doing more than God's?
Can we not hear our Mother complaining
that what we're adding to her blanket of insulation
is warming dangerously the whole works?
What would God think of stewardship's abdication
stemming from the deadly combination
of myopic religion and greed? 12/12/21

On a Twist of Fate

Lay low, anger,
wanting to clang the alarm once again
about blind humankind's greed
that imperils our singular home.
Be quiet, heart,
as you send out energy and light
to those whose lives were flattened by a tornado
that might on a twist of fate
as easily have flattened your own. 12/13/21

How hard on the heart with Afghanistan on the mind.

Engaged in Love's Practice

Safe houses in Kabul risking all
to help friends escape assassination--
imagine the terror of both hidden and hiding
with life literally to lose if detected.
How not be in awe at the courage
of those daily engaged in love's practice. 12/13/21

If the Aim is to Blame

You who castigate Biden
for bungling the getting out,
what about the decades-ago oil lust
of the greedy that got us in? 12/13/21

Howard Thurman was impassioned on few things more than this.

What is *Your* One Thing?

Sail your inner sea
until you find an island,
then search this island
until you find at its center an altar.
Standing next to this altar
is an angel with a flaming sword
allowing nothing past but one thing,
the one thing at the very core
of the *nerve center of your consent.*
What is *your* one thing?
Only this will the flaming sword
allow to be placed upon the altar
standing at the heart of the island
in your vast inner sea. 12/17/21

Early morning musing with pen at the ready.

Wakeful Dreaming

A puppy sleeps next to me
(of what might he be dreaming?)
as I sit this early morning
with pad in lap and pen in hand
poised to record what bubbles to the surface
from my own wakeful dreaming. 12/17/21

Taking after Whitman, I prefer compatible partners dancing to incompatible foes clashing.

Partners in the Dance

It would seem a contradiction
to plead Lord I am not worthy
that you should come under my roof
and in the same breath exclaim with Whitman,
I celebrate and sing myself!
until each is recognized as a partner
in the bold and baffling, dazzling human dance. 12/18/21

I can't ignore both my age and hers. Our time together is all the more precious for being limited. Come to think of it, is that not the case with our every relationship?

To Mari When I'm Here No Longer

Know that I consider it the tallest of blessings
to watch you beginning to flower.
None of this "cute as a button business"
(though that you decidedly are),
rather what I'm thinking instead
is the beautiful strength of your vivacious kind spirit!
It's part of the sadness of things
that I will seem to be absent from your future flowerings,
but I'm here to tell you, Miss Mari Finn Holland,
that I'll be with you still then!
All you'll have to do is be still
and remember wherever you are
Pop Pop is right there with you--
grandfather with his granddaughter,
hand in hand, heart to heart. 12/18/21

Getting down to basics.

Breathless with Appreciation

Having to stop more often to catch my breath
on my morning jogs to get the paper
leaves me breathless with appreciation
for the gratuity of each new breath. 12/18/21

The poem on page 97 of this volume sets the stage for the following.

A Broadening of View

A Buddhist's response to a poem I entitled "You":
"That the universe is awake and aware
with a consciousness that pervades all phenomena
is a staggering truth
that even scientists apart from the mainstream
are beginning to proclaim.
The ultimate 'Thou'
that engages one with total absorption
may not be the godhead
except as met without disguise or hesitation
in the consciousness of every other being."
Little compares with a broadening of view. 12/19/21

It's not something you forget when a visiting bishop says it right out loud from the pulpit.

And Why Not Jesus?

We wouldn't know Peter was married
had there been no mother-in-law mention--
likely the other apostles too given the cultural expectation,
and why not Jesus?
I remember Jack Spong's bold conjecture
that the wedding feast of Cana just might have been his own—
less puzzling then his mother's worry
that the wine might run out. 12/19/21

*Instead of outside pulling the strings, imagine God's ongoing cre-
ation an inside job, now enlisting our assistance!*

In the Image and Likeness

When chance things keep happening--
some bright, some dark, most in between--
where does God fit in?
Perhaps not the puller of strings
sending weal, permitting woe,
but instead the seed at the core,
the nerve center at the heart,
ceaselessly bent on turning chance into meaning.
From whatever befalls us today,
let God do her birthing thing--
make the meaning.
Could that not be what it means
that each is made in the image and likeness,
able to respond with gratitude to every brightness,
able to answer every darkness
with *Light let there be?* 12/20/21

Born on the equinox, conceived on the solstice—I'm still trying to wrap my head around it.

When the Seed of Me was Sown

That the night of my parents' loveplay
when the seed of me was sown
happened to be the longest of the year
gives one symbolically inclined much to think about.
To think of being launched in loveplay
on the winter solstice! 12/21/21

Quick hands, thank God, were at hand to meet the crisis.

Emergence of a Newborn Girl Wonder

Never in the life of two solicitous parents,
four hovering grandparents,
and an expectant world holding its breath
will the night of October 25, 2018
ever be forgotten for the dramatically frightful
but ultimately delightful
emergence of a newborn girl wonder. 12/24/21

Seeing the depiction I instantly recognized a kin.

Listening to Muse instead of Pharaoh

Sitting at the feet of his Pharaoh,
stylus poised over papyrus,
the scribe with back turned keenly listened.
Centuries later another of the same tribe
listens to Muse instead of Pharaoh
for what words to transcribe. 12/26/21

Pondering the departed.

A Gem from Harry Potter

Harry to the apparition of his parents:
"Why did you leave?"
"We didn't leave," they responded
pointing to his heart,
"We're here." 12/25/21

And Then They are Gone

People come into your life bathed in light
and then they are gone,
leaving you wrapped in both sorrow
and the abiding warmth of their light. 12/27 21

We Struck Something Deep

I'm giving myself over to a memory this morning
that widens the longer I linger.
He liked to be called Jimmy
and though our time together was brief
that I've carried him with me fifty years
tells you we struck something deep.
Pity not a life ending
when it helped propel another life forward.
A memory widens the longer you linger. 12/27/21

When Breathing Takes Leave

Short rapid breaths
and then the final.
It's surprising how a face empties
when breathing takes leave.
Twenty-six years ago this day
it emptied of her,
the face of my mother. 12/28/21

A wish to sisters and brothers as we all embark on a new year.

Never Yield to the Illusion

Imagine your life's mentors
who have sailed out of sight
having the chance to make their presence again felt
thanks to inhabiting now your heart.
You at the helm and they firing the engine
together are embarking on the voyage
of a pristine new year.
Never yield to the illusion
that you're a solitary craft fragile
sailing an immense ocean empty. 12/31/21

Looking forward and looking back.

Under Duty's Gaze

Noblesse oblige--
responsibility comes with privilege.
Shape-shifting Duty looks me straight in the eye
on the brink of a blank page new year.
What, I ponder tremulously under the gaze,
is my duty to write on it? 12/31/21

A Time for Harvesting

It's time to look back over the year just ended
to harvest messages received,
wisdom learned sometimes the hard way,
courage found at crossroads,
actions taken making a difference,
astounding gifts blowing in
from the blue wild yonder. 1/2/22

I'm always on the lookout for a beautiful question.

What is it You're Here to Fight For?

Consider that your warrior nature
is waiting to spring into action
in response to an unmistakable summons
from the nerve center of your consent.
What is it
more than anything else in the world
you believe you are here to fight for? 1/2/22

Every story can speak your name

Let Metaphor Liberate

Whether he really walked upon water
cease the useless debate,
let metaphor liberate.
Instead be heeding the call
to disregard whipping wind
and step out of the safety
of your own storm-tossed boat. 1/4/22

Would he even recognize the place?

Imagining Whitman Today

Instead of barbaric yowls
I imagine outraged cries
were Whitman here to witness
American democracy's demise. 1/5/22

Just wondering.

What if Nero
fiddling while Rome burned
had been the one to start the fire? 1/13/22

Reminders of the power of words of healing and kindness.

Is There a Heart Now Leaning?

"Speak but the word
and my soul will be healed"--
such faith in the power of the word!
Is there a heart now leaning
toward you in hope of hearing
a word of healing? 1/4/22

How Often It's the Unexpected

Think how often it's the unexpected
that makes your day.
Surprise another with your attention
and make her day.
Surprise another with your kindness
and make his day. 1/18/22

Bolster Another's Belief

Put aside for a moment
your worry and your grief.
Your smallest act of kindness
can bolster another's belief
that there's more to life
than worry and grief. 1/18/22

The quote to follow is from the late Jack Good's The Fortunate Ones: Beatitudes and Biographies. Jack was a wise man, eloquent speaker and writer, and, most treasured of all, a good friend.

The Attitude of a Beggar

Blessed are the poor in spirit
has long slipped into ho-hum,
but what about this?
"Fortunate are those with the attitude of a beggar...
It would be appropriate if the Beatitudes
were less popular and more feared." 1/20/22

When the realization sinks in there will never be time enough.

From a Calm Place of Being

Even if we strove a hundred years
we'd never be done with all that needs doing.
Perhaps then the goal is less to do than to be
so that from a calm place of being
would come clear the next thing
that needs doing. 1/23/22

What's with all the circlings?

Whirling Dervish of a Universe

Thinking of the great circlings--
sun around Milky Way's core,
planets around sun,
moon around Earth--
gets me wondering whom do I circle,
who circles me?
What is it, I further wonder,
about this whirling dervish of a universe
so enamored of circling? 1/24/22

How hope for the hunter without worry for the hunted?

Both Hope and Worry

Hearing a woodpecker search for breakfast
triggers both a hope he finds it
(it's cold outside and I, too, know hunger)
and a worry for his possible breakfast
hardly secure in hidden warmth
to hear nearby pecking. 1/24/22

Having Ira Progoff as a life guide has been one of the graces.

Automatic Recalibration

"In a profound sense there is no such thing
as making mistakes on the spiritual dimension of life.
All our experiences feed into a single inner process
that self-adjusts as it proceeds.
At each point it establishes a new condition of balance,
and this takes us an additional step along our way."
No chiding here for making a wrong turn,
simply an invitation from Ira Progoff--
attentive to apparent mistakes and roads not taken--
to trust our internal GPS
guiding from a starting point ever new. 1/27/22

Fear need not have the final word.

Terror Precedes Taking a Leap

No, no, no I can't!
I'm not cut out for it,
simply don't have it in me.
Besides, wouldn't falling flat on my face,
freezing up,
being a laughingstock fool
way too much be disruptive to my life?
Surely somebody else (*anybody* else)
must be more suited.
My no is getting weaker.
Spirit of the daring Universe, be my strength,
keep reminding me I do have it in me.
Yes, I can! 1/28/22

An invitation to slow down and listen.

Imagine What Words

Imagine there is Someone
who knows everything about you--
pitch dark and bright shining,
Mouse eager to shrink, Moose eager to bellow--
cherishing both who you are
and who you have it in you to become.
What words might that indwelling Someone
be speaking to you now? 1/28/22

Would I could remember this when fierce winds start blowing.

Safe Home

Presence penetrates,
animates,
enfolds—
unthinkably an It, absolutely a Thou.
Could anything be more comforting,
more emboldening,
than finding in Presence safe home? 1/29/22

The eye-opener for me was The Peaceable Kingdom by
Jan de Hartog.

Incandescent Realization

I thrilled to realize that my gravitations
to Native American and Quaker spiritualities
were *but one gravitation.*
Incandescent realization. 1/29/22

Just think of one whose words have altered your life!

Wand in Wizard's Hand

Visiting the Dickens Museum in London
stunned me with the force of the man,
the power and reach of his words that still stand—
think Scrooge and remember hope!
Pen indeed is mightier than sword,
wand in wizard's hand. 1/29/22

Once again loving holds the key.

The Deepest Most Heartening Thing

Don't throw away immaculate,
just extend its possibility beyond Jesus and Mary.
Hopkins hewed to the essence in his kingfisher sonnet:
"I say more: the just man justices,
Keeps grace: that keeps all his goings graces..."
If in the moment we are kind,
how are we not immaculate
as long as we *continue* being kind?
But Hopkins wasn't finished:
"Acts in God's eye what in God's eye he is--
Christ--for Christ plays in ten thousand places,
Lovely in limbs, and lovely in eyes not his
To the Father through the features of men's faces."
When we limit immaculate to Jesus and Mary
we miss the deepest most heartening thing!" 1/30/22

Does not friendship trump just about everything?

I'll Just Tuck Him in My Heart

Zoom allows you to magnify a figure
to fit the whole screen.
I'm now pondering a man's face
possibly nearing the end of his race
who thanks to his integrity, kindness and humor
has for decades embodied for me grace.
When the time comes to let him go,
I'll just tuck him in my heart
and take him everywhere with me.
You tell me, what comforts and emboldens more
than a friend at the core? 1/30/22

How Could I be Afraid?

Come meet Lame Deer, seeker of visions:
"How could I be afraid
with so many people living and dead helping me?"
We are covered by fear and sadness
when we imagine ourselves alone. 2/1/22

A case could be made for the eight holiest days of the year.

In Close Accord

Show me someone who celebrates
not only solstices and equinoxes
but cross-quarter days between each
and I'll show you someone in close accord
with the loveliest of Mothers.
Candlemas is almost here
when Winter clasps Spring! 1/31/22

Wei wu-wei—thank you, Alan Watts, for long ago opening a door.

Non-action Igniting Action

Let go and let God.
"How yawn inducing, vapid, hackneyed, pitifully passive--
move on, for God's sake, to something more fresh,
energetic,
riveting,
forceful,
imaginative,
calling for high heroism!"
I think you missed it.
Here it is again but sweep away the cobwebs
and this time *listen*:
Let go AND LET GOD--
residing in the very core of you--
propel you into action your dullard self never dreamed!
What drama could be more compelling --
never knowing what heroic action
God will call out of you next? 2/2/22

The occasion was a Zoom presentation by a local defense attorney.

Reinforced

When you approach a presentation
trusting you may gain some useful knowledge
but come away with wisdom instead,
let's just say you've been reinforced
to keep seeking knowledge but trusting
more than knowledge may be in store. 2/2/22

Faith in the Judicial System

You'll not likely regain faith in the judicial system
by reading a book on law,
but you just might when you encounter
an attorney for the defense
who against all odds has never lost it. 2/3/22

The Last Thing Expected was a Sermon

Struggling to find words
for what drew him to his work,
he stammered it likely had to do
with his love for the underdog
like Jesus for the poor and imprisoned.
The last thing expected was a sermon,
but a sermon was given. 2/3/22

As for the kind of day you will have, doesn't it depend on who takes control?

Two Views on the New Day

Mouse:
Groan, not another day.
Beside the aches and pains
it's the worries colliding in the night,
and now fresh dispiriting news
of all the world sadness.
How will I get through it?
Moose:
What is mine and mine alone
to make happen today
so I can smile this evening looking back
on having emphatically made
a small but real difference?
What opportunity another day! 2/7/22

It's a hard thing to do, to imagine aging alone.

Much Harder for Those Aging Alone

A fall yesterday
luckily left me with only a sore wrist
plus a bruise on the behind.
Not getting any younger I'm bracing myself
for more falls coming.
Easier said than done to age gracefully
even when help is at hand.
How much harder, I find myself wondering,
for those aging alone? 2/7/22

I remember knowing nothing about Harriet Tubman when Black
History Month began. Now there was a pitiful ignorance

How Glad, How Sad

How glad for the praise for Black History Month
opening minds and hearts willing
to centuries of amazing courage and achievement.
How sad for the disdain for Black History Month
from minds closed and hearts hardened
against even wanting to gain knowledge
of centuries of amazing courage and achievement. 2/7/22

I bet you could find sixty in your house too.

A Manner of Pest Control

It was this day, I smile to remember,
long ago when hitchhiking in Ireland
that the felicitous idea came in a flash
to create my own mythology.
It was Steinbeck who sowed the seed
saying he had given the name Welsh rats
to his chronic nibbling worries--
it seemed to help him berate himself less
when the pesky rodents were at it again.
Said seed found fertile soil
as within but a few days
I had named at least sixty occupants
in the house I call me.
Call it introducing a manner of pest control
with imagination and humor combining
to reduce self-berating. 2/10/22

Getting some mileage from a quote from Thoreau.

Know Your Own Bone

"Do what you love.
You have two homes, your body and the planet.
Know your own bone,
gnaw at it,
bury it,
unearth it and gnaw it still.
Know your own bone!"
Watching our puppy guard his bone
hints what Thoreau was getting at--
is anything more important? 2/7/22

Two Bodies

You have two bodies,
your own and the planet.
Get head and heart around that
and next time you hear "climate crisis"
the scales will fall from your eyes
as you scream bloody murder
for the assault on your body! 2/8/22

Royalty in Disguise

Imagine the whole sweep of the cosmos
to be an elaborate preparation for the arrival
of the royalty in disguise
looking out through your eyes.
Let it sink in--
never before has the universe
seen exactly what you see! 2/8/22

Matt Cook will never cease traveling with those blessed to have known him.

Gone from Us but Not Gone

To learn that a beloved friend
gone from us but not gone
has now a bench in his honor
in a beautiful park in Chicago
with a plaque carrying words
reflecting his deep love of trees--
all this brings a warm realization
on a cold morning in Virginia.
While I may be far from Chicago,
unable to sit on his bench,
I'm never far from trees
among whom I will walk slowly, bow often,
remembering a beloved friend
for whom there's a bench in Chicago,
gone from us but not gone. 2/11/22

February only seems dull when you miss his song.

Shake a Leg, Lazy Bones

Can't you hear him, February singing?
I'll grant it's still cold hereabouts
but isn't it clear from the lengthening light
that Winter's hold is relaxing?
Feel Earth stirring from her long silent slumber
at February's insistent call:
"Shake a leg, lazy bones,
start throwing off the covers.
Spring in short order will be sprung! 2/11/22

February 12th always means it's time to remember.

Think Where We'd Be

Abe Lincoln was born today
thirteen years and two centuries ago.
Think where we'd be
if that boy raised in obscurity
hadn't risen from obscurity
not only to save a nation
but to be an exemplar of humanity.
"With malice toward none, with charity for all"--
we honor you, Father Abraham,
on this holy day of your birth. 2/12/22

And here you thought you couldn't sing.

Find Your Song

Learning *Bhagavad Gita* means the Song of God
gets me thinking this chilly morning
before a woodstove's cozy burning.
If God is singing and I am a child of God,
could that mean when you hear me singing
you're hearing God?
Before you call me grandiose
consider for an astonishing moment
that the same applies to you.
Find your song
so God again can be heard singing. 2/12/22

Naming one's gift
feeds fuel to the flame--
are we not each a living flame? 2/12/22

No attempt here to be impartial.

Long Live Scribes

We would never know of Rumi
had scribes not recorded
what that dervish entranced
sang while he danced.
Long live scribes and their scribbling. 2/12/22

Surely a poet can find better things to follow than football, right?
Wrong.

How to Apply This Loftiness?

D-Day for the Bengals
gets me thinking of Krishna's advice to Arjuna
concerning his apprehension on the brink of battle:
Follow dharma's call,
give it your all,
let go fretting about outcome.
Hmm, how to apply this loftiness
to the imminent battle at hand
ponders a lifelong Bengals fan? 2/13/22

On the Eve of Super Bowl

I can't imagine Great Mystery
cares a hoot who wins a big game
but does care absolutely
about effort toward excellence
and respectful manner of engagement.
What difference would it make, I wonder,
if in my outer or inner contests
I was attached not to outcome
but to effort toward excellence
and respectful manner of engagement? 2/13/22
It won't be hard to detect I was prepared for the worst.

Hearkening to Jesus before the Big Game

Remembering Jesus was for the underdog
brings a smile to this Bengals fan,
and if the dream crashes in the end,
won't Jesus be hard to beat
for a guide in facing defeat? 2/13/22

The next two are for all sports fans, regardless the sport.

In a Flash a New Exemplar

Pay close attention when viewing sports.
In a flash you may have a new exemplar
for how you hope to meet
your own moments of tall reach
regardless if ending in defeat. 2/13/22

Fitting Metaphors

Instead of disdaining sports
for distracting from causes more momentous,
see them as providing fitting metaphors
for harnessing body, mind and spirit
to apply to causes more momentous. 2/13/22

A chilling essential read is Timothy Snyder's On Tyranny.

Straight from the Fascist Playbook

What struck me in a book on tyranny
was how much in Hitler's rise to power
he used rallies to whip the aggrieved to a frenzy
for what had been *stolen from them*. 2/13/22

If all you see at the UN is the Meditation Room created by Dag Hammarskjold, the trip will have been worth it.

Word-Markings

Here I am
thirty years beyond turning fifty
seeing each day as prologue
to a new mountain to climb
hoping to leave behind
word-markings for future climbers.
Thank you, Dag, you live still. 2/15/22

Natural selection and the second law of thermodynamics leave out something elemental.

Natural Uncanny Propulsion

What Darwin couldn't account for
when tracking incremental variation
was the mysterious inner propulsion
igniting also prodigious leap.
Instead of natural selection
he might have called it natural uncanny propulsion
carrying both the incremental and the prodigious
all the way to you and me.
And where to from here,
where the next prodigious leap?
Given the mystery behind natural uncanny propulsion
there's no telling. 2/15/22

I'm all for morning vitamins to fortify the day.

Be Fortified

Preparation: prayer;
conditioning: contemplation;
mind-training: meditation.
For coming combat be fortified. 2/15/22

Deep attention anchors.
Best be ready, held steady.
Stormings never cease. 2/15/22

Looking back on a turning point.

You Won't Stop Me, Neurosis!

At a crisis moment in my life
forty-two years ago to the day
anxiety was such that complaints from my body
insisted I wave a white flag,
run the hell away.
But what I wrote that evening in my journal--
"You won't stop me, neurosis!"--
signaled come hell or high symptom
I would *not* run away.
Victories of spirit occur on battlefields
never more than when the battle is within. 2/15/22

Moose eager to let loose, don't we each have one?

Are There not Times to Smash Silence?

"Hello!" was the safest word I could think
to hurl into the open clearing
to remind myself I not only have a voice
but a strong one!
Though no one was within earshot
still it took a small act of courage.
"Who is this Yankee causing commotion,"
I imagined some hidden one thinking,
"by smashing an Irish evening's silence?"
But a small victory is still a victory,
and I look back on that HELLO long ago
as a critical crossing of a threatening threshold.
Are there not times to smash silence,
to hell with what anyone thinks? 2/16/22

In all the world
is there a stronger gift than trust.
to give or receive? 2/16/22

When it comes to piety, what can match that of plants?

Bordering on Adoration

Turning each amaryllis daily
to compensate for their bending toward the light
calls from me admiration
bordering on adoration
for the piety of their incessant bending
toward the luring light. 2/16/22

How is an echocardiogram not a subject fitting for a poem?

Examinations of the Heart

Tomorrow I get the results of a test
that examined the chambers of my heart,
not unimportant for a guy of 80.
It strikes me my morning ritual
whether before woodstove or sunrise
is but a different kind of examination of
the chambers of my heart. 2/16/22

Assorted haiku

I am an enthusiast
waiting for the next thing
to light my eyes! 2/17/22

How can melancholy
not have a chamber
in the house of my heart? 2/18/22

The poem of now
is right before our eyes--
ah, if only we could read. 2/18/22

No prize awarded
for reaching eighty
except all the memories! 2/19/22

How could I have launched skyward without a sure foundation?

Never Will I Rue My First Garden

I mean no disrespect to the church of Rome,
spirit garden for my first 31 years,
forever the foundation.
I mean no disrespect as I remember this day
on O'Connell Street in Dublin
forty-nine far-flung years ago
when scales fell from my eyes and all I could see
were fireworks fitting for an independence declaration.
Never will I rue my first garden
foundation for all flowerings to follow. 2/18/22

The speaker happened to be John Yungblut, but that's not the point.

Your Last Sermon, Preacher?

"How I wish I could preach again
for I have got hold of a prophecy!"
Inquire not who said it,
rather imagine these words are your own
as your prepare for your curtain to fall.
What truth above every other
in your search across a lifetime
stands out incandescent?
What is your own barbaric yawp, matching Whitman's,
to shout over the roofs of the world?
Your last sermon, preacher,
the congregation leans in to listen. 2/20/22

The great give-away prayer of Ignatius begins with the Latin word "Suscipe" (pronounced Sushipay)--hence the name I gave to the mountain I daily look out on.

To Think over Half My Life!

How anniversaries quicken spirit,
invite homage to memory.
Forty-one years ago today,
then 39 (now 80) I moved in with my love to Cor Mundi,
home of our dreams on the land of our longing.
To think I've looked out over half my life
on Mt. Suscipe at the heart of the world! 2/21/22

How can "Have no fear" not come from vast personal acquaintance with fear?

Imagine the Battles to Get There

Hearing a friend last evening
speak with awe of his fearless grandmother
struck awe in me too
imagining the battles she must have fought
to get there. 2/22/22

*Going to sleep with Beethoven on my mind led in the morning to
these next two.*

Pondering the Possible Connection

Thinking of the gifts he left behind,
that force of nature we call Beethoven,
and then being reminded of his life's frightful suffering
gets me pondering the likely connection
between extraordinary gifts and extraordinary suffering.
Perhaps the two come with the territory
when one heeds a fierce calling.
Aspiring to follow your bliss?
Remember in French "blesser" relates to being wounded.
2/23/22

Pulling Back from the Brink

Reminded that no less than Beethoven
pulled back from the brink of self-erasure
so he could give his gift to the rest of us
calls to mind a despondent Lincoln
refusing to toss in the towel at a dark impasse
lest he have nothing substantial to leave behind
marking that he was here.
Who knows how many,
mindful of gifts not yet given,
have pulled back from the brink
to the world's grateful aggrandizement? 2/23/22

If only we could quit arguing over names, and get to the essence.

Carry Flowers to Her Shrine in Your Heart

There's a sanctuary on Hawaii's Big Island
honoring Lono, Goddess of Forgiveness,
where any seeking can find refuge and pardon.
Carry flowers to Lono's shrine in your heart,
trusting you too will find there refuge and pardon.
Likely you address her by a different name,
perhaps Sophia or Isis,
perhaps Kwan Yin or Mary. 2/24/22

If it's been a while since visiting Whitman, consider this an enticement to revisit.

Whitman, Mystic

"I celebrate myself, and sing myself"--
you'd be excused for thinking Whitman egotistical
until remembering the next lines.
"And what I assume you shall assume
For every atom belonging to me as good belongs to you."
Substitute mystical for egotistical and you'd come closer
to hitting the nail on the head. 2/26/22

Recognize the reality—for good reason we no longer feel immune.

Doubt Not It Could Happen Here Too

Watching refugees flee the takeover in East Ukraine
fearing for their homes and their lives
wrenches the heart.
Doubt not it could happen here too
were a fascist to hold sway
trusting laws of the land
with cronies strategically at hand
could be blown away. 2/26/22

I've long contended that these two were the stand-outs in 19ᵗʰ century America.

What Set the Bells Ringing

When reminded recently that February
was the choice for Black History Month
because of the birthdays of Douglass and Lincoln,
you could tell from the eyes in my face
that bells in my head were ringing. 2/26/22

February 26, 1986—now there was a musical day.

Bopping to Beethoven

My daughter I'm sure doesn't remember
for she wasn't yet 2
but having just read Beethoven's biography
and with her in my arms
I danced thirty-six years ago today
to every one of his symphonies!
Watching her fingers on a recent visit
still dance across the keyboard,
maybe down deep she *does* remember. 2/26/22

One thing led to another.

Three Things Called to Mind

Listening to my dog gnaw his bone
calls Thoreau to mind:
"Know your own bone, gnaw at it,
bury it, unearth it and gnaw it still.
Know your own bone!"
Which calls to mind Lincoln urging Grant:
"Hold on with a bulldog grip,
and chew and choke!"
Perhaps it's less getting a grip
than remembering who grips us.
Which calls to mind the Hound of Heaven
said to be ever on the scent. 2/27/22

It's been an eagle brother exchange, thirty-five years and counting.

A Ritual and a Wild Notion

Here's a ritual to keep a month ending
from drifting into oblivion.
Looking over calendar or journal,
write in a letter to yourself
things of importance, outer and inner,
that hadn't yet surfaced in your life,
enriched or challenged your life,
an exact month prior.
Imagine having a dozen of such letters
to look back on at year's end
in order to reap the year's harvest.
And if you're up for a wild notion,
imagine the impact it would have on a friendship
to exchange such letters monthly,
capped by a summation by each at year's end
of his friend's 12-month spirit-journey. 2/28/22

Aiming for a bit of perspective

Things Would be Worse

Whatever your complaints
about the state of American affairs,
imagine were Trump still commander-in-chief
what he'd be assuring us about his pal Putin.
Let's just say things would be worse. 2/27/22

Watching a Zoom presentation brought him back to life.

Marveling at Technology and Frederick Douglass

I encountered Frederick Douglass last evening
and never had to leave home!
Granted technology complicates our lives
by encroaching on our time in nature,
but think too of the undeniable expansions.
And on the subject of technology and expansion,
go order a book of Douglass's speeches
to discover an opulent room in literature's mansion. 2/28/22

May they rest in peace.

Perilously Close to Egregious

I wasn't the black sheep--
never doing anything egregious--
but rather the *lost* sheep
wandering from the straight and narrow.
Come to think of it,
for devout Catholic parents to see their once pious son--
good God, he was almost a priest!--
incomprehensibly fall by the wayside
must have for them come perilously close
to egregious. 3/1/22

Just an old guy musing.

Ready or Not

Years back I wondered
if I'd be ready to go at 80--
after all that's quite a journey.
Well son of a gun I made it
and now wonder if I'll be ready at 90.
Ready or not it some day will end,
this incredible journey. 3/1/22

Seldom are things black and white.

Muddying the Water

No defense here of Putin, clearly reprehensible,
but might not Russians have a grievance
when assurances that NATO would not expand
were blatantly discarded?
Given a history of foreign encroachment,
have they no reason to worry?
This does not excuse invasion,
just muddies the water. 3/1/22

Anyone taming, and being tamed by, an animal knows better.

Cross-Species Love

Instantly dropping his bone
Buckley runs to Penny in the morning
when she rises to greet him.
Those scoffing at talk of cross-species love
are sorrowfully deluded. 3/2/22

When will we ever learn?

> Pitiful species--
> marching again to war
> knowing full well it's hell. 3/2/22

Is it love pushing or love pulling? A case could be made either way.

A Gardener of the Spirit Singing

> Think the implication of love's push and pull
> by envisioning the living universe
> as a seed yearning to flower.
> Check out Teilhard de Chardin
> to hear a gardener of the spirit
> sing of it. 3/2/22

A red-letter day in the life of a graced man.

Blown Away by Her Radiance and His Blessing

> On the day of the birth
> of the light of my life
> I marvel at the reach of her mind,
> the workings of her hand,
> the kindness of her heart,
> the lyricism in her soul,
> the incandescence of her presence in my life.
> Excuse the rapture of a man
> blown away by her radiance and his blessing. 3/3/22

My attempt here is to honor the absolute compatibility of wild chance and deep meaning.

Meant for Me

To say she was meant for me
is not exactly to say she was sent to me.
Call it a wild happy chance
that when she passed my way
something deep-down discerning
leapt to the sudden intimation
that this apparition in a graduate psychology class--
of a young lady with hair down and blue dress
looking straight in my eyes and smiling--
could, who knows, maybe some improbable day
be the very one meant for me. 3/3/22

Impulsive or preplanned, that is the question. Either way, he was in for it.

Troublemaker

Whatever your definition of a troublemaker,
by overturning those tables in the Temple precinct
Jesus qualifies.
Knowing both the brutal occupiers of the land
ready to squelch any rabble starting to rouse
and the religious powers that be
infuriated by the impudence of this self-proclaimed prophet
with the gall to call into question their authority,
could he have been surprised by what was coming? 3/4/22

Easier said than done, but it might sow a seed.

A Strategy for the Self-Berating

If hard on yourself in the evening
for what you've failed to get done during the day,
try focusing on one thing that *did* get done
and precisely because of you!
It's less easy to beat up on yourself
when savoring your advancement of creation. 3/4/22

Kazantzakis thought the best definition of God might be Ah!

Flames in woodstove,
snow outside falling—
could awe be the reason we're here? 3/12/22

Jung called them synchronicities. Strict materialists scoff,
but what if?

Flukes or Hints?

Amazing coincidences—
flukes devoid of meaning
or hints from a mysterious universe
bent on new revelation? 3/12/22

Closing your eyes, you can almost feel the push and the pull.

Titanic Forces

Pushed by past,
pulled by future—
what energies in this pulsing moment! 3/12/22

It's a very good thing we can't see what is coming. Whatever it is we can only pray we'll get through it, together.

Dark Skies Thankfully Brighten

An exact year ago today
my grandson was rushed from the ER
to the children's oncology unit,
the dreaded diagnosis coming the next day.
The challenges of the year can only be guessed,
the generosities of the year can only be blessed,
as dark skies thankfully brighten. 3/12/22

Just think of the times we can look Sun in the face!

Looking Sun in the Face

The only times of the day
we're able to look Sun in the face
are soon after its rising
and just prior to its disappearance.
No wonder are dawn and dusk,
East and West,
each steeped in holiness—
arms-outstretched welcoming,
reverent head-bowing adieu. 3/13/22

A simple response when you ask me why I write.

> Words pulsing on page
> will speak when I'm gone.
> I am hoping not to leave. 3/14/22

A heartening invitation.

> Think of the heart's beating
> as the drumbeat of love
> for those residing? 3/14/22

I had considered Sue Monk Kidd's The Book of Longings to be her most ambitious and courageous book for telling a story of the imagined wife of Jesus. Upon rereading The Mermaid's Chair, another candidate swims into view.

Sympathetic Gray

> Given the cultural conditioning,
> judgment is ever ready to jump in
> on subjects deemed black and white—
> infidelities of married woman and man of cloth,
> father's choice to make his exit,
> others' choice to assist him
> and then have to carry the smoldering secret,
> and finally the self-mutilation of one of these
> turning to mythology to bear it.
> It takes imagination and courage
> to paint subjects deemed black and white
> in rich texture of sympathetic gray.
> Welcome, any on the lookout for sympathetic gray,
> to *The Mermaid's Chair.* 3/16/22

It was Joseph Campbell who quoted Nietzsche, leaving me wondering since.

This is What I Need

When faced with great misfortune
Nietzsche declared, "This is what I need!"
To think of welcoming what assaults us
to my ego is ludicrous.
And yet.
What if the present anxiety
(come to think of it, when is there *not* one?)
indeed were a disguised friend,
precisely what Moose welcomes
to let loose the force of his bellow?
Poppycock! Mouse squeaks
with his abiding streak of yellow. 3/17/22

In the next two I found myself wondering, what to do if the worst comes?

When Our Hearts Can't Bear It

What better can we do
when our hearts can't bear it
than turn to a friend?
Not one of us
can bear alone crushing. 3/18/22

When I Scream

Some losses so crush
that we scream we can't bear it.
Should it happen to me
I pray to be held by a friend of the heart
when I scream. 3/18/22

Even anniversaries that pierce carry comfort.

Tucked Deep in Our Heart

Anniversaries of great loss
pierce for bringing the pain back
but also shine to remind us
of whom we now carry
tucked deep in our heart. 3/18/22

How challenged to the core when looked up to.

Prayer for Fortification

I am awed to realize
knowing my flaws better than any
that I am looked up to as father of hope,
grandfather mountain,
trustworthy guide,
lasting friend.
I pray every day to be fortified
as I try to live up
to such awesome designations. 3/18/22

May this help them to relax for whom the words just don't come.

Trust you give comfort
with your eyes and your arms
when you can't find the words. 3/19/22

Safe to say the equinox was on my mind for these next two.

Erotic Equinox

Twice in the year's gracing
night and day coil
in rapturous embracing. 3/20/22

Two Days Alone

Farewell Summer, hello Autumn,
farewell Winter, hello Spring—
two days alone
in the sweep of the dance of the year
pause in the balanced perfection
of their day-night communion in passing. 3/20/22

Ever since seminary days, this metaphor has stayed front and center.

Paul's Great Metaphor

Each one,
member of the divine living body—
Paul's great metaphor! 3/20/22

Isn't every reader on the lookout for beautiful sentences?

Each word a sparkling gem—
what stunning necklace
when beautifully strung! 3/22/22

Think of the Annnunciation story as a fiery conjuring to help us imagine the igniting of flames, not restricted to the flame Jesus.

The Danger of Sitting in Silence

Some depictions of the Annunciation
have Mary dropping her book upon hearing
the upending by a message from an angel
of her life as she knew it.
An illiterate peasant
she was likely just sitting in silence
wondering what might pop up next,
just as we ourselves might be wondering
when similarly engaged in the dangerous activity
of sitting in silence.
Depending how we respond to what we hear,
our lives, too, could be upended. 3/25/22

Watch Out for What You Read

While Mary likely was not reading a book
prior to an angel's intrusion,
each of us might be
so watch out for what you read.
The lightning thrust of a message
just might impregnate you with new life,
but only if you answer the attempted penetration
with the full measure of your consent. 3/25/22

Staying with the Annunciation a little while longer.

Has Logic Ever Conceived Possibility?

Those who dismiss the story
of an angel's stunning announcement
and a young girl's startling submission
as patently untrue
have logic on their side,
but you tell me,
has logic ever conceived possibility?
Have you never followed a hunch,
taken an audacious wild leap
which turned out to make all the difference?
Lay aside logic on occasion
and be flabbergasted to imagine
in Mary's story your own
should you ever find the courage
to say YES to a summons
from wherever. 3/26/22

How deny the undeniable? Just cry "Fake news!"

The Power of Propaganda

That a sizable number of Americans
loathe Biden more than Putin
bespeaks the power of propaganda
to cloud mind,
harden heart,
turn truth on its head.
Who cares about truth anyway? 3/26/22

And after John must come Jesus!

How Dare He Call for Repentance

Off the school shelves
must come books about the Baptist—
his disquieting call for repentance
might threaten kids' self-esteem
not to mention their parents'! 3/27/22

*Speaking of books that might be coming off the shelves for inviting
discomforting self-scrutiny, here's one by Howard Zinn.*

An Unvarnished Look

For an unvarnished look
at what happens to the little guy
in the basement of the shining house on the hill,
check out *The People's History of the United States.*
Those revering the varnished version
of the home of the brave and the land of the free
will disdain even to touch it
unless perhaps to throw it on a pyre. 3/29/22

The little lion in question, really looking like one, is actually a Pomeranian puppy by the name of Buckley.

A Tender Morning Ritual

When little lion stands on my chest
looking me square in the eye
with his paw patting my face,
the message is unmistakable.
"Enough already with the quiet, let's run!"
I let him know if I'm not ready
with the slightest shake of the head
and a whispered "not yet,"
but guaranteed in two minutes
said little lion will be back patting my face.
Such unmitigated elation
when he gets a nod of the head instead.
"Alright already, let's run!" 3/30/22

What makes an airport holy? The arrival from the other side of the world of a son in your arms.

Thirty-three years ago
he landed in waiting arms—
four lives transformed! 3/31/22

BIOGRAPHICAL INFORMATION

Charlie Finn lives with his wife Penny north of Roanoke near Fincastle, Virginia. Both are retired and enjoying their life in the country, which includes tending to woodpile and many gardens. Their love of traveling takes them to visits with their children April and Adam in Tennessee and Texas, as well as to enticing points beyond. While Finn retired in 2015 from a 40-year career in counseling, which followed seven years as a high school English and Humanities teacher, he has not retired from his lifelong love of writing. His published writings included the following:

Circle of Grace: In Praise of Months and Seasons (1995)

Natural Highs: An Invitation to Wonder (1999)

For the Mystically Inclined (2002)

Contemplatively Sweet: Slow-Down Poems to Ponder (2004)

Earthtalks: Conjectures on the Spirit Journey (2004)

The Elixir of Air: Unguessed Gifts of Addiction (2005)

Deep Joy, Steep Challenge: 365 Poems on Parenting (2005)

Earth Brother Jesus: Musings Free of Dogma (2005)

Embraced It Will Serve You: Encounters with Death (2006)

If a Child, Why Not a Cosmos? Lovesongs to Earth and Evolution (2006)

Fuel for War: Patriotic Entrancement (2006)

Earth Pleasures: Pets, Plants, Trees, and Rain (2007)

Ithaca is the Journey: A Personal Odyssey (2007)

Steppingstones to the Civil War: Slavery Integral to Each (2008)

Aging Liberal Nostalgic for Vision (2008)

Empathy is the Key: Toward a Civil War Healing (2009)

Gentle Warrior John Yungblut: Guide on the Mystic's Journey (2009)

Full Heart Singing: Letters and Poems to a Girlchild (2009)

The Mastery of the Thing!: Transcendence in Counseling and Sports (2010)

Crafting Soul into Words: A Poet Sings of the Journey (2010)

Please Hear What I'm Not Saying: A Poem's Reach around the World (2011)

Roots and Wings: Gifts from Parents (2012)

John Yungblut: Passing the Mystical Torch (Pendle Hill Pamphlet #417, 2012)

Building a Memory Cathedral: Wisdom Figures (2013)

Building a Memory Cathedral: Years, Decades, Months (2014)

O the Mind, Mind has Mountains: Searching for the Heart of Hopkins (2015)

Mandalas Serving Memory: New Ways to Celebrate Your Life (2016)

New Under the Sun: Fecund 2016 (2016)

Focusing on Just One Gift: One Hundred Selected Poems (2017)

Great Day in the Morning: One Hundred Selected Poems (2018)

Sixty to Sing Of: A Wealth of Guardians (2018)

Winter Offerings: Poetry and Prose Dancing (2019)

Mining for Gold: Climbing Mount Empathy and Reclaiming the Mystical (2020)

Witness to the Unvanquished Human Spirit: Poetry for a Troubled Time (2020)

Who's to Say Every Bush is Not Burning?: Poetry during the Pandemic (2021)

Blue Plums on a Mat of Leaves: Ponderings at Break of Day (2023)

Information about many of Finn's works can be found on his website, www.poetrybycharlescfinn.com. Inscribed copies can be ordered through him at either charlesfinn@ntelos.net or charles.c.finn@gmail.com.

9 781734 480757